The Buddha—
A True Revolutionary

VEN. POMNYUN SUNIM

The Buddha—
A True Revolutionary

혁명가 붓다

Through the Buddha's Eyes,
Through His Life

JUNGTO

Through the Buddha's Eyes,

Through His Life

The Greatest Revolution

Preface

●

Meet the Revolutionary Buddha

The Buddha was born and lived on the Indian subcontinent about 2,600 years ago. Why do we need to revisit his life today? In our free democratic society, we often take for granted individual human rights and a world without discrimination based on gender, race, or class. However, the reality 2,600 years ago was entirely different. Women were subjected to strict hierarchies and discrimination in a male-dominated society, and social status was rigidly divided between masters and servants based on class. The concept of individual human rights was virtually nonexistent, and many people were even denied basic survival.

People of that era believed that their fate was determined by the will of the gods or by their karma from past lives. Within this fatalistic mindset, people believed that making offerings and performing rituals to receive divine blessings was the only way to escape from suffering. The Buddha grew up in this historical context. However, around the age of twelve, while accompanying his father to the Spring Planting Festival, he saw a bird eating a worm unearthed from the soil and wondered, "Why must one die for another to live? Isn't there a way for all to coexist?" Additionally, seeing farmers suffering from harsh exploitation, he questioned, "Why must some people sacrifice so others can live in abundance? Is there no way for all to be happy together?"

He posed these questions to his teacher, who responded dismissively, "That's useless thinking. Only by winning in competition can one survive." Education at that time focused on training individuals to become victors, and losers were simply expected to endure their fate. Thus, the Buddha renounced the world in search for the truth of life. Through profound enlightenment, he discovered the truth that "Everything in the world is interconnected." Going beyond the extreme teachings prevalent at that time, "Follow your desires" and "Suppress your desires," he presented the Middle Way, "Being aware of desires as they are."

Furthermore, the Buddha challenged the prevailing social norms that regarded men as inherently superior to women and the priestly class as sacred while the servant class was deemed inferior, preaching they were false beliefs. He taught that only by breaking free from these false ideologies could people perceive the truth and recognize the inherent equality of all beings. The Buddha proclaimed that one's fate was neither dictated by divine will nor predetermined by past karma, but that we can be free from all suffering by escaping ignorance and attaining enlightenment.

From today's perspective, the absence of gender and class discrimination seems natural. However, in ancient India, such ideas shook the very foundations of the existing social order and beliefs. That is why I want to call the Buddha not just a "great teacher" but a "revolutionary" who transformed the world. From this perspective, I decided to change the title of my previous book, "The Human Buddha, His Great Life and Teachings," to "The Buddha: A True Revolutionary," emphasizing that he was a revolutionary who transcended the limitations of his time and forged a path to a new world.

The Buddha's teachings did not remain confined to

individual enlightenment; they gradually gained acceptance among broader segments of society. During King Ashoka's era, they even had a significant influence on mainstream society. However, as time passed and Indian society became increasingly feudal, with heightened class and gender discrimination, Buddhism also began to drift from the Buddha's original teachings, influenced by the prevailing trends of the time. Originally, Buddhism was a teaching about awakening from ignorance and attaining nirvana. However, it gradually became more religious in character, and it prioritized seeking blessings and securing a favorable rebirth after death rather than individual freedom and happiness. As a result, ordained practitioners took on the role of priests performing religious rituals, and lay practitioners became simple devotees praying for blessings, making Buddhism indistinguishable from other religions.

Today, we live in an era of material abundance, yet spiritually, we find ourselves increasingly impoverished. What we need in this era is not Buddhism as a religion centered on praying for blessings, but rather the wisdom the Buddha attained in reality as a practitioner, and the way of life in which he practiced it. The Buddha's specific teachings, imparted through conversations with those experiencing suffering, provide valuable insights for addressing the crises facing modern civilization, such as the loss of humanity, the collapse of community, and the destruction of the natural environment.

Therefore, rather than focusing on Buddhist philosophy, this book examines the Buddha's life and how he manifested his wisdom in the social and historical context of his time. I hope that readers will reflect on the Buddha's life and consider what insights his teachings can provide in solving the problems we face today. May this book, in some small measure, help foster a new perspective for overcoming the limitations of modern civilization.

April, 2025, Seoul
Ven. Pomnyun Sunim

Contents

Chapter 01

In a Life of Abundance, Anguish Begins

The Ganges River in Varanasi

01.
The Birth of the Buddha

●

Examining Our Suffering

People often advise against discussing religion and politics with family and friends, as differing opinions can lead to arguments. However, I would like to talk to you about Buddhism. What I want to discuss is not Buddhism as a religion but rather the Buddha as a human being and the life he lived as a practitioner.

You may wonder why I want to talk about a person who lived 2,600 years ago. The reason is that there are similarities between the issues the Buddha faced during his lifetime and the challenges people face today in the modern world. I thought that examining the Buddha's life might help us solve the problems of today. That is why I want to share the story of the Buddha as a practitioner.

Today, we live in a time of great material abundance. If people from 100 years ago were to see us now, they would likely have a hard time understanding why we are suffering. They might ask, "Is there no food to eat? Are there no clothes to wear? Is there no place to sleep? You don't have to cook with firewood, wash clothes in the river, or walk long distances. So, what exactly are you suffering from?

Yet, we still don't feel like we have everything. Things have certainly improved compared to the past, but we always think life is hard because there is always something lacking. We worry about what to eat, what to wear, and where to sleep. We live under a great deal of stress in modern society.

I started elementary school in 1960, and at that time, Korea's GDP per capita was around $100. Today, it is said to be $35,000. Materially, that's a 350-fold increase. But has our happiness increased by 350 times? Or even 35 times? Have we at least become three times happier? While it's true that our living conditions have improved significantly compared to the past, it's hard to claim that we are even three times happier. Even now, we believe that if the economy grows, if we earn a little more money, or if we have a bigger house, we will be happier. But there's no guarantee that if our GDP per capita becomes 10 times higher, say $350,000, the suffering and stress we experience today will be resolved.

In the past, much of our concern was about food, clothing, and housing because there weren't enough of these necessities. Now, although society has solved many economic problems and achieved democratization, it still doesn't seem to make us truly free and happy. Of course, there are still many issues that need to be addressed, like building better social safety nets for the disadvantaged and granting more autonomy to citizens. But will solving these issues lead to true happiness and freedom? Reflecting on our past, even if the economic and social conditions improve in the future, it's difficult to say for certain that happiness will increase.

●

Siddhartha:
Anguish Amidst Abundance

How should we live? A young man named Siddhartha Gautama asked this question about life 2,600 years ago.

Siddhartha Gautama was born a prince in a small kingdom. Even 2,600 years ago, as royalty living in a palace, he did not lack for food, clothing, or shelter. He ate good food, wore fine clothes, lived in a beautiful home, and enjoyed a materially prosperous life.

One day, as Siddhartha was passing by on horseback, a woman sang a song:

"How happy must a woman be to have such a person as her son? How happy must a woman be to have such a person as her husband? How happy must a woman be to have such a person as her father?"

At that time, women had no rights or authority. A woman's happiness was determined by the men in her life—being born to a good father, marrying a good husband, and having a successful son in her old age. During such an era, Siddhartha, with his high status and privileged position, was admired by many women as an ideal father, husband, and son.

Nevertheless, Siddhartha Gautama was deeply troubled, much like many of us today. If he had lacked food, clothing, or shelter, he might have prayed to the gods for help, as was customary at the time. However, Siddhartha's suffering could not be resolved through prayer. He had no choice but to constantly ask himself, "Why am

I suffering?" Siddhartha's suffering while living in abundance in the palace 2,600 years ago, and the suffering of the people living in material abundance today, may stem from similar existential questions.

Even today, some people still pray to a higher being for help or for material gain, though less so than in the past. The number of people who follow a religion is now smaller than those who don't, and the number continues to decline. In particular, the younger generations have far fewer religious adherents compared to the older generations. This isn't necessarily an indication that religion is failing; it suggests that if religion is about praying and receiving something from a higher power, the need for young people to engage in such practices has decreased in today's society.

If our current suffering cannot be solved by obtaining something external, we must seriously ask ourselves, "Why am I suffering?" What led the young Siddhartha to ask this question while living in a palace? According to the sutras, Siddhartha's doubts began when he attended the Spring Planting Festival at the age of twelve. Until then, Siddhartha had been raised within the palace grounds and had two teachers: one taught him humanities subjects like philosophy, religion, and art, while the other focused on governance, military strategies, and martial arts, which were essential knowledge for a king to be. Siddhartha excelled in his studies, was healthy, and had a natural talent, so overall, he was a promising young man. In today's terms, he came from a privileged background, was intelligent and healthy, and attended a top university.

According to the customs of India at that time, children were educated by their teachers until the age of twelve to fifteen. After that period, when they became adults, they inherited the family profession and were trained by their fathers. In the year Siddhartha turned twelve, he participated in the Spring Planting Festival with his father, King Suddhodana. To become a king, he had to follow his father and learn everything.

When Siddhartha went out of the palace with his father for the first time after completing his studies with his teachers, he was shocked to see how people lived. The farmers, who were plowing, were emaciated, covered with dirt, wearing tattered clothes, and their faces were contorted with pain. They looked very different from the people Siddhartha had seen in the palace.

Siddhartha asked the farmers, "Why are you living in such misery?" The farmers replied that they had no choice but to live this way due to the oppression and exploitation by the officials or landowners. India at the time had a strict class society where 90% of the population were slaves. Farming was the work of slaves, so at the farming festival, Siddhartha witnessed the miserable lives of the slaves.

Until then, Siddhartha had lived comfortably in the palace, assuming that everyone lived in a similar way. But when he ventured outside the palace, he realized that was not the case. At that moment, Siddhartha became vaguely aware that the comfort he had enjoyed was not simply given to him but was made possible at the expense of others' suffering.

Siddhartha also saw a farmer whipping an ox as it plowed the field. He saw how people were continuously whipping the ox to make their work easier. The ox, foaming at the mouth, was working laboriously, and tears could be seen in its large eyes. Seeing this, Siddhartha wondered, "Why must one suffer such pain for another's comfort?"

As the ox pulled the plow through the field, the plowshare dug deep into the ground, exposing the worms beneath the soil. When the worms were uncovered, birds swooped down and pecked at them. Observing this,

Siddhartha wondered, "Why must one die for another to live? Is there no way for all to live together? Is there no way for all to be happy together?"

At the Spring Planting Festival, Siddhartha's father, the king, used a plow made of gold, the ministers used plows made of silver, and the commoners used plows made of iron. However, Siddhartha did not participate in the festival. Instead, he sat under a tree, deeply contemplating, "Why must one die for another to live?"

The king wanted to show his son the great prestige of a king through the farming festival, but Siddhartha was nowhere to be seen. After the farming festival ended, the king searched for his son but could not find him. Since it was the first time he had taken his son outside the palace, he grew worried and searched everywhere. Eventually, he found Siddhartha meditating under a jambu tree. The sight of his son meditating appeared so holy that the king instinctively bowed to him.

Siddhartha, who had always been bright and cheerful, looked gloomy and deeply lost in thought and meditation after returning to the palace from the Spring Planting Festival. When his worried father asked him what was troubling him, Siddhartha asked questions like "Why must one die for another to live? Is there no way for all to live together? Why does one have to lose for another to win? Is there no way for everyone to win together?" Neither his knowledgeable teachers nor his loving, powerful parents could provide an answer to these questions.

Up until then, whenever Siddhartha asked a question, his teachers would always provide an answer, which he learned from. But no one could answer his questions. Instead, they told him that he was dwelling in useless thoughts, so Siddhartha had no choice but to explore these questions on his own through meditation and contemplation.

Siddhartha's father, the king, thought that his son was acting this way because he was still young and hadn't yet experienced the pleasures of the world. Since his son had become an adult, the king thought that if he enjoyed the pleasures of singing and dancing and being with women, he would forget everything. So, the king often arranged banquets for Siddhartha to indulge in such pleasures. However, even while enjoying the banquets, Siddhartha would suddenly recall the large, tearful eyes of the ox or the image of the farmer in ragged clothes. Whenever this happened, he would quietly leave the banquet hall and sit alone to contemplate and meditate. Things didn't go as his parents had hoped.

In the end, the king arranged Siddhartha's marriage and later appointed him to govern a region of the kingdom, hoping this would help his son adapt to reality. However, despite making some progress, Siddhartha would repeatedly fall back in anguish. This ultimately led to Siddhartha's decision to renounce the world.

Siddhartha was neither a divine being like a god, who is the object of faith, nor was he a figure destined to become a Buddha through countless lifetimes of practice. To discuss Siddhartha's anguish is to examine this young man, who was born into the world and experienced suffering just like the rest of us, found the path to truth, attained enlightenment, and spread his teachings to free people from suffering.

It's impossible to understand a person with the explanation that they were destined for greatness or had to become that way because they accumulated a lot of merit in their past lives. A person's character is influenced by the environment in which they grew up. Family dynamics, social and historical contexts, and the natural environment all influence the formation of a person's character.

From this perspective, we need to understand the

customs, ethics, and the natural environment of India in which Siddhartha Gautama grew up. We also need to know the political, economic, social, and cultural situation of the time in order to grasp why this young man had such anguish.

Today, there are many advanced fields of study. For instance, in cultural anthropology, if there is a record that one was "born from an egg," research is conducted to find out what that expression means. Cultural anthropologists study many similar cases in the world to discover what it means. We will examine the life of Siddhartha with a comprehensive approach that includes the perspective of cultural anthropology.

Tracing the footsteps of the Buddha who lived as a human being, we will try to find out how we can live our lives more freely, happily, and meaningfully while doing something significant in the world. The goal is not to discuss a specific religion, but simply to bring a person from 2,600 years ago into the present and have a conversation with him.

02.
India's Natural Environment and History

●

A Look at India's Natural Environment and History

To understand the life of Siddhartha Gautama, we first need to know about the natural environment and historical background of the Indian subcontinent where he lived.

The Indian subcontinent is one of the cradles of the world's four great civilizations and the birthplace of the Indus Valley Civilization. India is surrounded on three sides by the sea: the Arabian Sea to the west, the Bay of Bengal to the east, and the Indian Ocean to the south. To the north lie the Himalayan and Hindu Kush mountain ranges, and to the northwest is the Thar Desert, geographically isolating it from the outside world.

This environment contributed to the development of a unique civilization.

The regions where the world's four great civilizations emerged were mostly arid grasslands. In the Neolithic and Bronze Ages, stone axes and knives were the primary tools. These stone tools couldn't cut down trees, only grass, which is why human civilizations mostly started in grasslands rather than forested areas.

Many ruins of the Indus Valley Civilization have been discovered in the Indus River Valley, and the people who created this civilization are known to be the Dravidians, the indigenous people of the Indian subcontinent. Traditional Dravidian beliefs included the concept of "reincarnation," the idea that people are reborn after death. The Indus Valley Civilization eventually disappeared after being conquered by foreign invaders.

Around 3,500 years ago, in 1500 BCE, the Aryans, a Caucasian tribe living in present-day Afghanistan, migrated south across the Hindu Kush mountains and the Pamir plateau into northern India, the present-day Punjab region of Pakistan. Some of them moved westward, becoming the Western Aryans, today's Europeans. Others moved eastward, becoming the Eastern Aryans who created today's Indian civilization. The Indus Valley

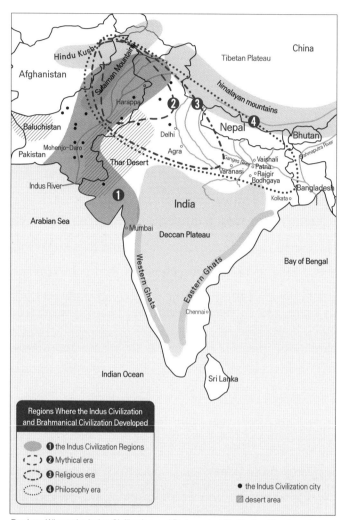

Regions Where the Indus Civilization and Brahmanical Civilization Developed

Civilization, created by the indigenous Dravidians, disappeared, and the current Indian civilization began with the Aryans. Therefore, the current Indian civilization can be called an Aryan civilization. The Ganges River Valley was a forested area, and its development was made possible by the advances of the Iron Age civilization. This is similar to how iron technology contributed to the development of the Yangtze River region during the Spring and Autumn and Warring States periods (770-221 BCE).

The Aryans were able to conquer the indigenous people along the Ganges River Valley and develop the forested plains because they had acquired iron technology.

●

The Emergence of
Religion and Philosophy

When the Aryans initially lived in the Punjab region, they sang songs called the Veda, praising the gods of nature. This period is known as the "Vedic Age" (1500-1000 BCE). The Aryans conquered the indigenous Dravidians and enslaved them, absorbing their culture, including the ideas of karma and reincarnation.

As the Aryans took over the Indo-Gangetic Plains along the Ganges River Valley, social classes gradually emerged. As people's occupations and roles diversified, these became established as classes. This period is called the "Age of Religion" (1000-800 BCE) or the "Age of Brahman." Among the Aryans, the priestly class who performed rituals for the gods were called "Brahmins," and the royal and warrior classes who ruled the world were called "Kshatriyas." Those engaged in economic activities such as commerce and agriculture were called "Vaishyas," while the conquered Dravidians were enslaved and called "Sudras."

The Aryans created myths to rationalize this class-based social order. They believed that the creator god Brahman created the universe and human beings. When creating humans, he created the Brahmins from his breath, the Kshatriyas from his side, the Vaishyas from his abdomen, and the Sudras from his feet. This creation myth established the class system, which is called the "caste system." In India, there were the "Chandala," or untouchables, who were excluded from the caste system. People avoided contact with them, believing their work to be impure, and they were not even regarded as human beings. On the other hand, the priestly Brahmin class was considered sacred and held the greatest power. It was believed that victories in wars were achieved through the power of the gods, which the Brahmins could invoke.

As the Aryans conquered most of the Hindustan plains, a period of peace arrived around 800 BCE. During the era of conquest wars, the focus was on performing rituals to win wars, but as peace arrived, people naturally began to engage in contemplation. This era of contemplation (800-600 BCE) is when various philosophical and religious texts, such as the Upanishads, were compiled. Hence, this period is called the "Age of Upanishads."

During the Upanishadic period, through deep contemplation, Indians ascribed philosophical significance to Brahman, the deity believed to have created the universe. They believed that within each human being, there resides the Atman, a part of Brahman. If humans discovered their true nature, Atman, they would be no different from god. This is called "Brahman-Atman unity," meaning that the fundamental essence of the universe (Brahman) and one's true self (Atman) are one and the same. This state is also called "liberation" from all suffering. This is because Brahman was thought to be pure, sacred, constant, and unchanging—free from suffering and filled with joy. Due to the concept of Brahman-Atman unity, they believed that by discovering the pure, noble, and eternal Atman, one could live free from suffering and experience only joy.

However, during the 6th century BCE, when the Buddha appeared, India was in a period of upheaval, with its long-standing peace shattered as various kingdoms vied for dominance. At that time, there were about 300 large and small kingdoms on the Indian subcontinent that were being unified through wars. In comparison, it could be likened to the Spring and Autumn period or the Warring States period in China. Around the time of the Buddha's appearance, the unification process led to the emergence of large kingdoms that could be considered empires. The first Kingdom to emerge was Magadha, followed by the rising new empire of Kosala. Along with these two, there were a total of 16 prominent kingdoms, collectively referred to as the "Sixteen Great Kingdoms" (Mahajanapadas). It was an era marked by war and chaos.

While the two newly risen empires, Magadha and Kosala, vied for supremacy, significant economic development occurred. With the advancement of the Iron Age civilization, agricultural production increased greatly, and as trade between countries developed, wealthy merchants emerged. Initially, the Aryans conquered the native Dravidians and made them slaves, and as more people were enslaved through wars, the number of slaves continued to increase. As a result, agricultural production through slave labor greatly increased. Naturally, cities emerged, and trade flourished between cities. With the increase in trade, wealthy merchants emerged from the Vaishya caste. Also, due to frequent wars, individuals with absolute monarchical power emerged from the Kshatriya caste. Consequently, the absolute power held by the Brahmins naturally weakened. The Brahmins were reduced to the role of performing rituals and blessings for kings and the wealthy. These shifts in Indian society gradually began to erode the rigid caste hierarchy.

Moreover, with constant warfare, killing became commonplace. Princes often resorted to killing dozens of their own siblings to claim the throne. It is said that among the kings of Magadha and Kosala, one ascended to the throne after killing over a hundred of his brothers.

Not only was there conflict and strife among the ruling class, but the gap between the rich and poor also became extreme. The children of the wealthy indulged in lives of pleasure. The Buddha himself experienced such pleasures in his youth, and many of his disciples from affluent families had similarly lived indulgent lives before realizing the impermanence and futility of such pursuits and taking refuge in the Buddha. In this time of chaos, it was difficult to understand and solve the problems of this turbulent world through the traditional teachings, beliefs, and philosophy of Brahmanism. If gods were indeed governing worldly affairs, it raised the question of why they allowed such disorder to persist.

●

The Emergence of
Various Philosophies Amid Chaos

The same logic applied to wars. When fighting against people of different religions, one might attribute victory to the protection of their own god. However, when Aryans who all believed in Brahman fought against one another, it became difficult to credit divine power for the outcome. Ultimately, the results of wars were determined by factors such as the size of the armies, the quality of their weaponry, and the effectiveness of their strategies and tactics. In this context, the influence of the Brahmins inevitably diminished, reducing them to their traditional role as priests conducting religious rituals.

Naturally, a new wave of thinkers claiming to correctly understand the workings of the world emerged. In ancient India, philosophers who opposed Brahmanism were called Samanas or Sramanas. While Brahmins naturally assumed the role of the priestly caste by virtue of their birth status, these new thinkers became philosophers not through their lineage but by leaving their homes, going into the forest, practicing asceticism, and promoting their own ideas. This act of leaving home for the forest was called "renunciation."

These new thinkers propagated various ideas about worldly affairs. Some asserted materialistic views, while others made extreme claims, such as stating that killing people is not a sin at all. They argued that if killing were a sin, kings should be punished; however, kings lived prosperous lives ruling over others, which, in their view, indicated that killing must not be a sin. These individuals, who introduced new philosophies or religions to provide alternative understandings of the world, were collectively referred to as "Samanas."

In Indian philosophy and spirituality, there were two groups: the mainstream thinkers, the Brahmins, and the non-mainstream thinkers, the Samanas. The mainstream Brahmins believed that if one wished for something, they could achieve it by borrowing divine power, and that wealth and status equated to happiness. Philosophically, this is referred to as "hedonism." On the other hand, the ascetic Samanas argued that one must suppress human desires in order to attain liberation, a practice known as "asceticism." The two groups each claimed that the path to liberation lies in hedonism and asceticism, respectively.

●

The Buddha Is Born
in Lumbini

It was against this historical background that Siddhartha Gautama was born and raised. In his childhood, he followed the teachings of Brahmanism, which were rooted in hedonism, and after renouncing the world, he joined the ascetic Samanas and practiced under teachers who practiced strict asceticism. The inner struggles of the young Siddhartha should be understood within this context. Without this background, we are left with a perspective that sees the Buddha only as a divine figure.

After attaining enlightenment, the Buddha rejected the notion that human destiny is predetermined. That is, he refuted the idea that fate is determined by the will of the gods, past karma, or the time and date of one's birth.

Today, Buddhism, as we know it, incorporates elements of traditional Indian beliefs, including the notion that one's present fate is shaped by past lives. However, the Buddha himself denied such fatalism. He taught his disciples that they should not engage in practices like face-reading, astrology, palmistry, or foot-reading to predict human destiny.

This stance is deeply connected to the background in which Gautama Buddha lived. The Buddha opposed fatalism, which rationalized suffering and unjust deaths as inevitable. Such fatalism ultimately justified the caste system and gender discrimination. The Buddha firmly rejected the idea that being born a woman or a slave was due to committing many sins in past lives. He opposed the caste system and gender discrimination, opening the path to enlightenment through practice and renunciation, even for slaves and women. Understanding the historical context of the Buddha's life helps us appreciate how revolutionary he was.

If we study Buddhism without understanding this background, we may end up accepting traditional Indian beliefs like fatalism and only view the Buddha as a divine figure. However, if we closely examine the life of the Buddha, we can see that he was someone who revolutionized the world.

Those who recorded the Buddha's life in later generations deified him, claiming that after countless lifetimes of diligent practice, he became a god in heaven and was eventually born into this world to become the Buddha. In the sutras, it is recorded that the Buddha was born from his mother's right side in Lumbini. Rather than seeing this literally, whether by thinking, "Of course, the Buddha could be born this way," or dismissing it as nonsense, we should view it symbolically. In Indian traditional culture, being born from the side symbolizes belonging to the Kshatriya class, meaning he was of royal lineage. It is also said that gods came and took care of the Buddha at his birth. This too can be interpreted as a portrayal, within the context of Indian culture, that he was seen as a being even greater than the gods.

It is said that the Buddha took seven steps immediately after his birth. The significance of this is that he went beyond the six realms of reincarnation. The six steps represent the six realms of reincarnation in traditional Indian culture. According to the karma one accumulates, they are reborn into one of the six realms: hell, hungry ghosts, animals, asuras, humans, or heavenly beings. This repeated cycle of rebirth is called the "six realms of reincarnation." However, the Buddha transcended these six realms and attained liberation, which is symbolized by his seventh step.

It is also described that he pointed one hand to the sky and one hand to the earth, saying, "In the heavens above and the earth below, I alone am the Honored One. As the three realms are full of suffering, I will rightly pacify them." The heavens refer to the realm of the gods, and the earth refers to the human world. The phrase "In the heavens above and the earth below, I alone am the Honored One" means that the Buddha is the greatest being in both the realm of gods and humans, signifying that he is above even the gods, the noblest being among gods and humans. This idea supports the concept of Buddhism as the most supreme religion.

Here, there is a phrase that we are not as familiar with: "As the three realms are full of suffering, I will rightly pacify them." This means, "The world is filled with suffering, and I shall liberate people from suffering." We should understand the phrase as a symbolic expression of the Buddha's entire life rather than a claim that he was destined to be the savior of the world. The Buddha was born as a human being, became free from the limitations of gods and humans, and showed all those who suffer the path to liberation from suffering. This is the symbolic depiction of the Buddha's life in the scene of his birth.

When the Buddha was born, the sage Asita is said to have prophesied upon seeing Siddhartha: "If he stays in the world, he will become a Chakravartin, a great universal monarch, but if he renounces the world, he will become a Buddha." Asita's prophecy reflected the hopes of many people who longed for peace and stability in a time when Indian society was in political, economic, and ideological turmoil. It expressed the ardent wish of the people that a great politician, a "universal monarch" who was a king of kings, would bring peace to the world.

At the time, there were many conflicting schools of thought, with 62 different views and 360 theories, each claiming to be true. Therefore, people hoped that an enlightened Buddha would appear to provide direction on what was right and wrong and the proper way for people to live. The "universal monarch" and "Buddha" can be seen as symbols of such aspirations.

Siddhartha Gautama did not follow the path of the universal monarch but chose the path of a Buddha. He awakened humanity from ignorance and showed everyone a way of life that leads to freedom and happiness. Two hundred years after the Buddha, King Ashoka appeared, uniting the Indian subcontinent and establishing peace. In India, Ashoka is referred to as the "universal monarch."

We must understand the young Siddhartha and the human Buddha within this historical context of India. We will now examine how the young Siddhartha grappled with anguish and sought the path of truth.

03.
The Anguish of
Young Siddhartha

●

Witnessing
the Contradictions of Reality
and Developing Profound Doubts

Siddhartha, born and raised in the royal palace, had no difficulty in terms of food, clothing, shelter, or daily living. He also did not experience significant conflicts in his relationships with his family. Of course, as history tends to be recorded from the perspective of the victors, it's possible that only the positive aspects of the Buddha's life have been preserved.

The young Siddhartha's inner turmoil began when he ventured outside the palace and encountered the many contradictions within society. He started to question the various inconsistencies he observed, but neither his teachers nor his parents could provide him with satisfactory answers, leaving him to ponder these questions alone. However, no one around him, including his parents, could understand Siddhartha's concerns. They could not comprehend why Siddhartha always agonized over these questions instead of enjoying the pleasures of the world like others.

During this time, Siddhartha ventured out through the northern gate and had a conversation with a Samana, an ascetic monk, which gave him new hope and a sense that there might be a solution to his inner suffering. This encounter led him to the decision that he, too, should renounce the world. But the first significant influence on Siddhartha's decision to leave the palace was the Spring Planting Festival.

At that time, life in India was divided into four stages. From birth to age 15 was the learning stage, where one would study under a teacher. From the end of learning to age 30 was the householder stage, during which one became an adult and inherited the father's occupation. After passing the family trade to one's son, the forest-dwelling stage lasted until age 45, during which one would live in the forest and focus on spiritual practice.

After the age of 45 was the wandering ascetic stage, during which one prepared for the end of one's life and went on a pilgrimage. While there were some variations depending on caste, each stage typically lasted about 15 years.

Following this tradition, when Siddhartha turned 12, he accompanied his father, the king, to the Spring Planting Festival. This was part of learning the role of a king and preparing to inherit his father's responsibilities. It was during this festival that Siddhartha began to deeply question, "Why must one die for another to live? Why must one be unhappy for another to be happy?" These profound doubts marked the beginning of his internal struggles.

●

Young Siddhartha's Anguish

As Siddhartha continued to grapple with the questions raised during the Spring Planting Festival, he reached adulthood without finding any answers. One day, he ventured outside the eastern gate of the palace, where he encountered an elderly man in a pitiful condition. The old man was frail, coughing up phlegm, barely able to walk, covered in wrinkles, and visibly in great pain. Of course, there were elderly people in the palace as well, so it was not Siddhartha's first time seeing an old person. However, the elderly person who shocked Siddhartha was an old slave abandoned on the street. While slaves were valued when young and healthy, once they became old or sick, they were discarded because the cost of treating them exceeded the price of buying a new slave.

Seeing the slave who was abandoned and unprotected due to old age, Siddhartha was deeply troubled. He wondered, "Is this what happens to a person when they grow old? Will I also end up like this?" He thought, "When young, people live differently based on social status, but when they get old, everyone ends up the same. If this is my future, how can I afford to laugh and enjoy life now?" With these thoughts, he returned to the palace.

Later, Siddhartha ventured outside the southern gate, where he encountered a severely ill person. The sick individual, abandoned and unprotected, cried out for their mother, father, and children.

Upon seeing this, Siddhartha went beyond simply

feeling compassion and the desire to care for others– he began to see the problem as his own. He thought, "Anyone can end up like this, including me." The portrayal of the old man and the sick person in the sutras shows the extreme misery people experienced when they became old and ill. At that time, slaves made up the majority of the population, and the sutras depicted the wretched lives of aging and sick slaves. Furthermore, based on the societal structure of that time, anyone who was defeated in war could be reduced to slavery, meaning this was not a concern limited to slaves alone.

One day, Siddhartha exited through the western gate and came across a corpse. The dead body, abandoned on the street, was being pecked apart by crows, creating a gruesome sight. Although the dead were usually cremated or buried, this was not the case for slaves. When slaves died, their bodies were discarded in the forest without any rites. There was a place in India where the bodies of dead slaves were dumped, called Sitavana, which translates as the "forest of corpses." Even today, when monks go to funeral homes to chant for the deceased, they say, "We are going to Sitavana." Sitavana is sometimes translated as cemetery, but since it refers to a dumping ground for corpses, cemetery is not an exact match.

We all have the right to die with dignity and have our bodies treated respectfully after death, but in those days, slaves had no such rights. Seeing this, Siddhartha gained a deeper understanding of the suffering experienced by people in the world, and he recognized that this could also be his fate one day.

Through these experiences, Siddhartha's reflections on the suffering of life grew deeper. His parents, recalling the prophecy of the sage Asita, became increasingly worried that their son might renounce the world and become an ascetic. In an attempt to keep him from leaving, they organized frequent banquets and even arranged his marriage, hoping he would find joy in worldly pleasures. They also built seasonal palaces called Triyashtirtha for their son, so he could enjoy himself in comfort throughout the seasons.

One day, Siddhartha ventured out through the northern gate and encountered an ascetic. Although the ascetic appeared emaciated and shabby, his eyes shone brightly, and he carried himself with great dignity. Through their conversation, Siddhartha felt a new sense of hope that he might find answers to the questions and doubts that had troubled him for so long. Thus, he decided to renounce the world and follow the ascetic path.

However, Siddhartha's parents were adamantly opposed to this idea. His father objected, and his mother tearfully begged him not to leave, so Siddhartha gave up the thought of renouncing the world. However, as time passed, Siddhartha's wish to renounce the world returned, and Siddhartha once again expressed his wish to leave home. This process repeated several times. His father, thinking that giving Siddhartha not only sensual pleasures but also the joys of governance might ease his distress, began to consider passing the throne to him. At that time, it was rare for a king to abdicate while still alive. However, since it was common for sons to stage coups to seize the throne if their fathers lived too long, Siddhartha's father misunderstood his son's anguish as dissatisfaction with not inheriting the throne quickly.

To appease him, the king gave Siddhartha control over a wealthy region called Gariṣa. However, when Siddhartha arrived there, he saw that the region's prosperity was built entirely on the harsh labor of slaves. He also witnessed the slaves cruelly whipping livestock to plow the fields. In response, Siddhartha ordered the release of all the livestock into the wild and commanded that the slaves be freed. These records suggest that the Buddha may have been the first person in history to put the liberation of slaves into practice. However, changing the entire social structure was impossible through the orders of a single ruler. Despite King Suddhodana's efforts, Siddhartha's inner anguish remained unresolved.

In the midst of this, Siddhartha's wife, Yasodhara, gave birth to a son. Siddhartha thought that his son would be a great hindrance to his future practice. In the Indian language, "hindrance" is termed "Rahula," which became the name of his son.

Some records describe that Siddhartha decided to renounce the world because he thought, "Now that my son has been born, if I remain at home any longer, I will never be able to pursue the path of truth." However, when we examine the historical and cultural context of India, it appears that there may have been additional factors. In India, inheritance rights are passed down only to male heirs. Thus, the birth of a son provided Siddhartha with a legitimate reason to renounce the world, as his son would now be the heir to the throne. In other words, having a son gave Siddhartha not only the justification for renouncing the world but also relieved him of the burden of filial duty to his parents.

●

Renouncing the World
in Search of a New Path

After the birth of his son, Siddhartha thought that there was a risk of becoming further entangled in worldly life and could no longer postpone his pursuit of the truth. However, since it was impossible to obtain his parents' permission, he had no choice but to secretly leave the palace at night. Before departing, he wanted to enter his wife's room where his son was sleeping and hold his son one last time, but fearing that his wife might awaken and prevent him from leaving, he opened the door, looked at his son, and left. This shows that Siddhartha's attachment and lingering feelings toward his child was greater than those toward his parents or wife.

Siddhartha left the palace with a firm resolution, determined not to return until he had found answers to his questions. He vowed, "Until I find the path that enables all people to live together in happiness, I will not return to the palace. Even if I die from poison or by falling from high palace walls, I will not return until I have attained the truth."

Fearing that the king would send someone to pursue him, Siddhartha rode his horse and crossed seven kingdoms. At that time, kingdoms were not large territories like today but were small in scale. Only after crossing seven kingdoms and a large river called the Anoma River did he feel confident that his father would no longer pursue him. He then ordered his servant Channa to return to the palace with the horse.

However, Channa did not follow Siddhartha's order and refused to return to the palace. If he were to return to the palace without his master, the crown prince, he could be executed as soon as he arrived for abandoning his master. Additionally, he couldn't imagine how the prince, raised in luxury, could survive in the dangerous wilderness, filled with wild animals and venomous insects. Channa tried to persuade Siddhartha to return. In response, Siddhartha handed Channa his crown and said:

"I did not renounce the world for personal gain or to go to heaven after death. I left to find the path that will bring happiness to all people. Tell the king that I did not leave due to any personal conflict or because I was deceived. I left in search of a way to free myself from suffering."

He conveyed the reason for his renunciation to the

king through Channa. After sending Channa back to the palace, Siddhartha grasped his hair with his left hand and cut it off with the knife in his right hand. Then, thinking that his clothes did not resemble those of a practitioner, he asked a hunter to exchange clothes with him. Thus, Siddhartha began his life as a practitioner.

For over a decade, Siddhartha had longed to become a practitioner and thought that, once he did, enlightenment would come quickly. However, even after one, two, three days, nothing changed. He was cold, hungry, bitten by insects, and constantly hearing the sounds of wild animals. He began to miss his warm bed and good food. Over time, he was plagued by regret and doubt. He grew so hungry that he tried to eat food discarded by villagers, but when he put it in his mouth, he immediately vomited. Siddhartha found himself regretting his decision to renounce the world and reproached himself:

"For over 10 years, I have longed to become a Samana and envied practitioners. But what am I doing now? After only a week as a practitioner, I am already full of regrets. I can't do this alone."

Thus, he set out on a journey in search of a teacher.

●

Searching for a Teacher

Realizing his own shortcomings and
ignorance, Siddhartha concluded it would be difficult
to practice alone, so he set out on a journey to find a
teacher. In a forest of ascetics, Siddhartha met an ascetic
named Bhaggava. Bhaggava and his disciples engaged in
extreme ascetic practices, such as hanging upside down
from trees, covering themselves with thorny vines, and
walking on boards studded with nails. They subjected
themselves to intense suffering. Compared to them, Siddhartha, who had thought his one week of practice in
the forest was hard, felt that he had been living far too
comfortably.

Meeting these ascetics strengthened Siddhartha's resolve to dedicate himself to spiritual practice. At the
same time, he was curious about why they subjected
themselves to such harsh ascetic practice. In response to
his question, the ascetics answered, "When a person is
born into this world, the amount of suffering and joy
they will experience in their lifetime is predetermined.
Therefore, if we endure the suffering in advance, we will
be reborn in heaven and enjoy blessings after death."

In essence, they were practicing asceticism to be reborn in heaven and enjoy blessings. However, Siddhartha realized that eventually, the blessings of heaven would be exhausted, and they would have to endure suffering again. This wouldn't be a way to escape reincarnation, the cycle of rebirth. It merely would postpone it temporarily. To keep enjoying blessings, one would have to continue practicing asceticism, which was a contradiction. Having spent 10 years contemplating these issues before renouncing the world Siddhartha quickly recognized the flaws in their reasoning.

Therefore, he left the ascetics and went to Vaishali, located about 350 km southeast of Kapilavastu, his hometown. There, he met a sage named Alara Kalama, who was a meditation master—a yogi, in modern terms. At first, Siddhartha found satisfaction in his practice under Alara Kalama and, within a few months, reached the same level of mastery as his teacher. However, while distracting thoughts seemed to disappear while sitting in meditation and focusing, they would return as soon as he moved or engaged in other activities. This made Siddhartha realize that meditation alone could not lead to complete liberation, so he left Alara Kalama.

Siddhartha set out to find an even greater teacher. He

met another meditation master named Uddaka Rama-putta in Rajgir, the capital of the Magadha Kingdom, which boasted the most advanced culture in India at the time. Siddhartha diligently practiced and soon reached the same level of mastery as his teacher. Although he attained a much deeper state of tranquility than before, he still found that this peace did not extend into everyday life—it was only maintained during meditation. Realizing this, Siddhartha decided to leave his teacher once again.

His teacher, recognizing that Siddhartha was a remarkable disciple, asked him to stay and co-lead the community. However, Siddhartha declined, saying, "I did not renounce the world to become the leader of a religious order but to find a way for all people to live without afflictions and suffering. I must continue to practice diligently."

With these words, he parted ways with his teacher. Five of his fellow practitioners, who deeply respected Siddhartha for his diligent practice, decided to join him. They too realized that there weren't any teachers left that they could learn from, and they needed to find the answers to the remaining questions themselves.

Siddhartha and his five companions traveled west, about 80 kilometers, to the village of Sena in Uruvela near the Neranjara River. This area is close to the ancient city of Gaya, near present-day Bodh Gaya. There, in a secluded and peaceful forest, Siddhartha and his five companions began six years of intense ascetic practice.

Chapter 02

SIDDHARTHA REALIZES
the True Nature
of the World

The Bodhi Tree near the Mahabodhi Temple in Bodh Gaya

01.

Siddhartha's Ascetic Practice

●

Discovering a New Path
through the Four Sights

As a child, my dream was to become a scientist, so I never imagined becoming a religious person. However, when I was in high school, I met a monk, who became my teacher, at Bunhwangsa Temple next to my school. Half voluntarily and half at the urging of my teacher, I decided to become a monk. I think I chose this path mainly because I found Buddhist doctrines to be scientific, logical, and rational.

However, Buddhism as a religion always left me with many questions. "Why is the Buddhism we see in reality different from what the Buddha taught?" So, I really wanted to visit India. Although 2,600 years have passed since the Buddha's parinirvana, I thought that if I could see the place where he had lived, I could understand him better. However, the opportunity to go to India did not come easily. After a few years, I finally had the chance to go. Since this was a long-held wish of mine, I arrived in India full of excitement. At that time, the airport in Kolkata had no jet bridges, so we disembarked directly onto the ramp. Overwhelmed with emotion at having arrived in India, I knelt and kissed the ground.

Despite the excitement and anticipation with which I arrived, the sight of the city of Kolkata was a huge shock to me. We were traveling like backpackers, staying in a small guesthouse in an alleyway. Although I had experienced poverty growing up in a rural area when South Korea was experiencing economic hardship, the poverty I saw in India was beyond my imagination.

One night, I went out alone to buy some water when a woman grabbed my arm and started speaking to me. I thought it was strange and tried to walk away, but she kept pulling me toward a light. She was holding a baby, and she kept moving her hand from the baby's mouth to its stomach repeatedly. I realized that she was saying the baby was hungry, so I followed her. She led me to a small shop that had goods displayed on the street and pointed to a can of baby formula.

"Oh, she is asking me to buy her the baby formula," I thought. In broken English, I asked how much it was, and the shopkeeper said it was 60 rupees. My heart sank when I heard the price. I remembered the advice I had received during my pre-trip briefing. I had been told that India has a currency unit smaller than the rupee called the paise and that, while it was okay to give beggars paise, I should never give them rupees. I had also been told that if we give more than a rupee, people, especially children, would follow us around, making it impossible to continue our travels. I had been warned multiple times not to give more than 1 rupee. So, when I heard 60 rupees, I was so surprised that I ended up running away. On the way back, I felt guilty for turning my back on a hungry child.

When I returned, I asked the professor who was guiding us, "How much is 60 rupees in Korean won?"

The professor smiled and said it was 2,400 KRW (2 USD).

At that moment, I was utterly shocked. "What? She was only asking me to buy baby formula for 2,400 KRW, and I reacted as if she was asking for my entire fortune and turned my back on her and ran away."

I felt immense guilt. I took some money and went back out to look for the woman, but she was already gone. At that time, I had been thinking a lot about helping the poor and advocating for social justice. But when I was actually confronted with a poor person, my reaction was completely different from what I had imagined. I was deeply shocked by this contradiction within myself. This experience became the catalyst for establishing schools and a health clinic for the "untouchables" or Backward Classes (BC) in India.

In downtown Kolkata, there was a very luxurious hotel. Our group went there for tea, and the walls and floors were all made of marble, and the teacups were plated with real gold. Inside the hotel, there were palm trees and a swimming pool. However, as soon as you stepped out of the hotel, there were poor people and people with disabilities begging on the street. I will never forget that sight. And I thought to myself, "When Siddhartha Gautama left the gates of his palace, could he have seen a similar scene to what I saw when I stepped out of this palace-like hotel?"

An adult might have either given the beggars a few coins or simply ignored them and walked away, but wouldn't a young boy inevitably have been troubled by such a sight? Wouldn't it have led him to either choose the path of competition to avoid ending up like those beggars, or consider how to find a way to achieve happiness together? The Four Sights are not just a story from the sutras but a problem we constantly face in our lives if we take a closer look.

I thought what I saw in Kolkata was the Four Sights. This is why, during my early pilgrimages to sacred sites in India and Nepal, I would always take a detour to visit the slums of Kolkata for a day. I believed that to truly understand what the Buddha agonized over, it wasn't enough to visit the historical sites; we also needed to experience the Four Sights ourselves. I believe that by investing our time and resources to travel to India and reflecting on the same questions Siddhartha faced, I think we can have a deeper and more accurate understanding of the Buddha's teachings.

"If Siddhartha Gautama were to come here today, what perspective would he have on the problems of the modern world? What struggles would he face as he contemplated these issues? How would he investigate solutions, and what path would he suggest for us to follow?"

We shouldn't think of the Buddha as a figure from 2,600 years ago, but as someone who is here with us now. Only then can we follow the Buddha's path. And even if you are not a Buddhist, I believe that modern people can gain valuable insight from a deep understanding of the Buddha's life.

●

Beginning
Ascetic Practice

After experiencing the Four Sights and embarking on the path of an ascetic, Siddhartha met various teachers, learning from them and practicing diligently until he reached the same level as his masters. One of his teachers, Uddaka Ramaputta, even offered him the opportunity to lead the community together. In that situation, any other person might have accepted the offer and stayed to exert leadership. But Siddhartha was different. He did not lose his initial resolve. Because he did not forget why he had renounced the world, he declined his teacher's offer and continued on the path toward enlightenment.

This event occurred when Siddhartha was in Rajgir. One day, from his palace, King Bimbisara saw a practitioner walking with dignity and focus. Curious, the king ordered his men to find out who the practitioner was and where he came from. When he learned that the practitioner was Siddhartha, King Bimbisara personally went to meet him in his chariot.

When King Bimbisara met Siddhartha and asked who he was, Siddhartha replied that he was from a small northern kingdom called Kapilavastu. King Bimbisara asked again, "Are you the prince who renounced the world?"

When Siddhartha confirmed this, the king made him an offer. "It is a great loss for someone as young and talented as you to become a monk. Come back to the palace with me. I have a sister you can marry, and together we can rule the kingdom of Magadha."

At that time, Magadha was the largest and most powerful kingdom in India. However, Siddhartha declined the offer. Thinking that Siddhartha was dissatisfied with the idea of co-ruling, King Bimbisara made an even better offer, "Then you take my place and rule this kingdom." Still, Siddhartha refused.

The king, thinking Siddhartha was reluctant to take over someone else's kingdom, made yet another offer. "I will give you a powerful army so that you can conquer other lands and create your own empire."

Siddhartha Gautama rejected even this offer and said, "Great King, I abandoned my own kingdom because I did not want to be king. Why would I want to have someone else's kingdom? I abandoned my kingdom, so why would I seize someone else's? Great King, I spat out the phlegm in my mouth because I have no need for it, so why would I happily swallow a large lump of phlegm that someone else has spat out?" With this, Siddhartha turned down all of King Bimbisara's offers.

Siddhartha had willingly given up his own throne, so he asked why he would want to take the throne of another kingdom, comparing it to discarded phlegm. Siddhartha firmly believed that he could not solve his anguish through worldly means. This conviction was the driving force that enabled Siddhartha Gautama to focus on his practice.

Recognizing Siddhartha's unshakable resolve, King Bimbisara said, "I understand. If you find the path you seek and achieve your goal, please return to Rajgir. I will serve you as my teacher and provide you with anything you need."

After parting ways with King Bimbisara, Siddhartha left Rajgir and entered the forest of Dungeshwari, near Gaya, where corpses were abandoned, and practiced diligently. Since the Buddha practiced here before at-taining enlightenment, it is called Pragbodhi Hill, which literally means "prior to enlightenment." However, the local name is Dungeshwari, which means "dirty land" or "impure land."

●

Engaged in
Extreme Asceticism

The Buddha practiced asceticism there for six years. He resolved, "I will undertake an effort that no one else has ever attempted." Even after learning as much as he could from various teachers, he had not ful-ly overcome his suffering. Therefore, he decided to take a path that no one in the world had ever taken. He did not avoid the cold, the heat, or even venomous insects. He gradually reduced the amount of food he ate. Ac-cording to the sutras, he ate one jujube fruit a day, then one every two days, and finally, one every three days. He practiced with such fearless determination until his body became so emaciated that he looked like a skeleton covered with a thin layer of skin. It is recorded that the shadow of death constantly loomed over him.

Whenever afflictions arose in his mind, he strengthened his resolve to continue his practice. According to the scriptures, Mara, the demon king, tempted him by offering the throne of a Universal Monarch if he abandoned his asceticism. Yet, Siddhartha did not yield to the temptation.

"I will not surrender. Your first army is greed, the second is anger, and the third is ignorance. I will not succumb to them."

The fact that Siddhartha did not waver even in the face of Mara's temptations means that he practiced with tremendous resolve and determination. At Sitavana, the forest where he practiced, low-caste children would sometimes come to search through piles of corpses for useful items or to graze their sheep. Seeing Siddhartha in the forest, the children would even make bets on whether he was dead or alive. That's how extreme his ascetic practice was.

Yet, even after six years of intense practice, Siddhartha had not attained enlightenment. He had done everything within his power, but he had not reached nirvana or attained enlightenment, so he must have been discouraged and disappointed.

At this point, Siddhartha reflected on his life. In his

youth, before renouncing the world, he had simply followed his desires. When he satisfied his desires, he felt joy and pleasure. This was the mainstream path, the way of the Brahmins. However, this path did not completely free him from afflictions. After renouncing the world, he chose the opposite extreme—denying and suppressing all desires, committing himself fully to rigorous asceticism. He practiced asceticism diligently in a state of tension, but this too was not the path to freedom and liberation. It is recorded in the sutras that the results of his ascetic practice during this time did not even reach the level of insight he had gained as a young man when he contemplated the question, "Why must one die for another to live?" during the Spring Planting Festival.

Although others saw him practicing extreme asceticism, his own state of mind was one of tension, not tranquility. Reflecting on his life, Siddhartha discovered a new path. He realized, "Whether I follow desires or suppress them, both result in unhappiness. Either way, it leads to suffering." Siddhartha Gautama had experienced the height of pleasure during his life as a prince and the height of asceticism during his six years of practice. And he realized that neither of these paths led to liberation.

●

Discovering a New Path,
the Middle Way

After six years of ascetic practice, Siddhartha reflected on which path truly led to nirvana and liberation. He realized that both following desires and suppressing them were extremes, neither of which led to liberation. He discovered a third path that transcended both, known as the "Middle Way." The Middle Way does not mean a "middle" in the literal sense but refers to the "right path to liberation."

Even before the Buddha appeared, terms like "Buddha," meaning "one who has realized the truth," as well as "liberation," "nirvana," "asceticism," and "Samana" were already used in Indian culture. However, the term "Middle Way" was first introduced by the Buddha. This third path, which involves renouncing both indulgence in pleasure and extreme asceticism, is called the "Middle Way."

The Middle Way is recognizing desires as desires without following them or suppressing them. It is recognizing desires as desires in a state of ease, without tension, suppression, indulgence, or resistance. After years of rigorous practice, Siddhartha discovered the path to break out of the cycle of both extremes and attain freedom from desires through the Middle Way. In other words, the path to truth is not found in indulging in worldly desires or in practicing asceticism. Many mistakenly think that truth can be found within the world or outside the world. The truth is found not in external circumstances but within our own minds. Upon realizing this, Siddhartha felt his tension dissipate, and his mind became calm and at ease.

Afterwards, he left the forest and went to the riverbank to bathe. While he was practicing asceticism, he had avoided bathing, believing it to be indulging in bodily desires. He also refrained from eating soft foods and never sat on anything comfortable. However, now that he had realized the futility of extreme asceticism, he no longer felt the need to adhere to such extreme practices.

He was so weakened from his ascetic practice that he collapsed on the riverbank while bathing and was carried downstream. Grasping a tree branch, he managed to pull himself out of the water. In Indian culture, where it is believed that gods reside in all things, this event was interpreted as the tree god extending its branch to save him.

A young girl named Sujata had come to the river bank to milk the cows and saw the collapsed ascetic. She was the daughter of the village head of Uruvela. She returned home and made a porridge-like meal called "milk-rice" and offered it to the ascetic. Siddhartha ate the meal and gradually regained his strength.

Seeing this, the five companions who had been practicing asceticism with Siddhartha decided to leave. They were disappointed to see him doing things an ascetic should avoid, such as bathing and eating soft foods. They thought, "Siddhartha has given up on practice. He wasn't able to escape his princely nature after all."

Until then, they had respected Siddhartha for his extreme ascetic practice, but when they saw him give it up, they were disheartened and left for another place. The evidence of Siddhartha renouncing asceticism was clear: he bathed, ate milk-rice, and sat on a mat of grass.

Left alone after his five friends departed, Siddhartha regained his strength and crossed the river to sit beneath a Bodhi tree to resume his practice. A shepherd happened to be cutting kusa grass nearby, so he obtained a handful of grass to spread beneath the tree and sat down. He sat comfortably and engaged in meditation.

The most important thing about the Buddha's six years of asceticism is that he practiced asceticism to the absolute limit of what a human can endure. When we give up on something too soon, we often feel regret, thinking, "I should have tried harder." However, the Buddha had practiced to the utmost extreme, so he had no lingering attachment to asceticism. This allowed him to discover the new path—the Middle Way.

The core teaching of Buddhism is the Middle Way. Historically, around the same time in other cultures, Confucius in China spoke of the Doctrine of the Mean, and in Greek civilization, Aristotle also discussed the concept of the middle path. However, while Confucius and Aristotle focused on the middle path in political matters, the Buddha spoke of it from the perspective of practice.

The Buddha discovered a new path that transcended both extremes—neither excessive nor lacking, not leaning toward either side. He found the most correct path, the "Middle Way," by turning away from both indulgence and asceticism. Through the practice of the Middle Way, he finally attained enlightenment. It was not through theory, but through his own experience that the Buddha discovered the Middle Way. Free from any hindrances, he followed the correct path, the path of truth, and diligently practiced it until he reached the final stage of enlightenment. In other words, the Buddha did not first attain enlightenment and then discover the Middle Way, but rather, he discovered the Middle Way, based on which he practiced diligently, and ultimately attained enlightenment.

02.
Attainment of Enlightenment

●

Practicing the Middle Way
in Your Life

After six years of asceticism, Siddhartha discovered the new path—the Middle Way. I first experienced my own Middle Way when I arrived in India for the first time. As I mentioned earlier, I had refused to buy formula for the Indian woman and her infant, which left me with an immense sense of guilt.

The next day, I started giving away all the money and clothes I had to the children begging on the streets, keeping only the essentials I needed for the trip. Soon, 20 to 30 children began following me everywhere I went. The people I was traveling with started criticizing me, saying, "How can we continue traveling like this?"

At the time, I had been so shaken by my encounter with the woman that I unknowingly began acting this way, but it ended up causing problems for my fellow travelers.

One day, while we were traveling, we stopped by a small tea shop on a rural road and had a cup of chai. There were a few children nearby, and I waved to them, saying, "Hey kids, come over here. I'll give you some candy." The children seemed like they were going to come but hesitated. When I approached them with a bag of candy, they ran away. Once again, I was shocked. At that moment, I realized, "Because tourists keep giving them things, those children are becoming beggars. I am the one who made them into beggars."

Seeing those rural children made me reflect on my actions. Even though the rural children were as poor as the ones in the city, since no one gave them anything, they didn't beg. From that point on, I decided not to give anything to begging children. No matter how much they asked, I refused to give them anything, thinking, "One piece of candy isn't going to change your life. In fact, that candy will only make you into a beggar. I am refusing to give you money for your own sake, not because I don't have any."

Later, when I visited the Sujata Stupa site near Bodh Gaya, I encountered a disabled boy who couldn't use his legs and walked with his hands. He kept following me, begging, "Bakshish, bakshish" (alms), but kept walking without giving him any money. But even when I told him to go away since I wasn't going to relent, he didn't leave and kept following me for almost one kilometer all the way to the Uruvela Kassapa site. At that moment, I found myself in a dilemma once again:

"Is it really the right path not to give anything to this person?"

I found myself in a situation where I could neither give nor not give. If I didn't give money, I would be seen as a stingy person ignoring the poor. On the other hand, if I gave out of pity, it might only serve to satisfy my own conscience while risking turning the children into beggars. Caught in this dilemma, I became deeply troubled.

While wrestling with these thoughts, I visited the place where the Buddha had practiced asceticism for six years. On the way up the mountain, there were countless children begging along the path. I turned to my companions and asked, "Is today Sunday?"

They replied, "No, it's not Sunday."

I asked again, "Then why aren't these children in school?"

They responded, "There's no school for them here."

"How can there be no school when there are so many children?" I asked again, but the only response I got was that there was no school for the children in that area.

After descending from Pragbodhi Hill, I had a conversation with some of the village elders about the situation in their community, and an idea came to mind. It was a way to help poor children without encouraging them to beg. The idea was to build a school where they could study. That's how we began building a school.

I proposed an idea to the village elders: "I'm a monk from a foreign country and have no children, but this is your country, and these are your children. Shouldn't you contribute something too?"

They said they had nothing and couldn't contribute anything. So, I asked the villagers to donate some land to be used as a school site. Ten villagers came forward and each donated a small portion of their least arable land. Seeing this, people joked, "Sunim went to the poorest village and managed to get donations." Anyway, that's how I worked together with the villagers to start building a school for the children.

Thirty years have passed since I founded the international relief organization, Join Together Society (JTS). Now, there is a hospital, two elementary schools, one middle school, and fifteen preschools, providing education to over 2,000 children every year. All education, medical services, and other support are offered free of charge.

Looking back now, my actions toward the beggars I encountered when I first went to India were not entirely wrong in the long run. Of course, I reflected deeply and regretted not buying formula for the woman who begged for her baby when I first arrived in India. On the other hand, my behavior of giving indiscriminately to the begging children, despite my good intentions, sometimes led to unintended negative consequences. However, it was through these experiences that I came to think about building schools for the poor children in India.

When we built the schools, it wasn't a one-sided act of charity. We collaborated with the local community: the residents provided the land, and JTS covered the cost of building materials. The locals also participated in constructing the school building, cooking meals for the workers, and working together to create the school.

It wasn't about unilaterally helping the poor, but joining together to work toward a shared goal. This process of finding a way that fit their situation was, for me, an experience of the Middle Way, learned during my travels.

The Middle Way is not a predetermined path. It is about continually seeking the most appropriate course of action without falling into extremes. In my Dharma Q&As, I don't offer fixed solutions. I listen to people's situations and offer advice that suits their circumstances and helps them find relief from their suffering. I believe that's the essence of the Buddha's teachings—the Middle Way. In Buddhism, how much knowledge one has accumulated is inconsequential. Even if it's a partial solution, what's most important is the attitude of continually exploring and finding solutions to the problems that arise in our everyday lives.

•

The Cycle of Joy and Suffering

Having discovered a new path and perspective, the Buddha did not return to Pragbodhi Hill where he had practiced extreme asceticism. Instead, he went to the Bodhi tree (originally called the Pippala tree, it was later called the "Bodhi tree" after the Buddha attained enlightenment) on the other side of the river. He sat under the Bodhi tree on kusa grass provided by a shepherd and practiced diligently. Unlike before, the Buddha no longer practiced with firm resolve, determination, or tension. He sat in a state of full awareness and relaxation, entering deep meditation under the Bodhi tree.

As his mind became more stable and his consciousness clearer, three temptations arose. These temptations are described in the sutras as being caused by Mara, the Demon King of the Sixth Realm, who is said to govern the highest heavens in the celestial realm. In Indian cosmology, the highest heaven is called "Paranirmitavasavarti" or "Desire Realm," which is ruled by Mara, whose world is one where all desires are fulfilled as one pleases. From a practitioner's perspective, Mara represents a force that hinders practice, which is why he is often referred to as the "Demon King."

One day, Mara's heavenly palace began to shake, prompting Mara, the lord of that realm, to look down at the human world. There, he saw a tiny being, seemingly insignificant as a speck of dust, striving to free

himself from all desires and cravings that all living beings possess. Mara realized that if this being became free
from desire, the world built upon desire would collapse.
Alarmed, Mara sent his three daughters to stop him.
Appearing as the most beautiful maidens in the world,
Mara's daughters tried to tempt the Buddha into abandoning his practice.

"You are so young, and on a beautiful day like this,
with flowers blooming and birds singing, why should
a practitioner sit alone and meditate in the forest? If
you die here, who will even know? Youth comes only
once and never returns. So, why not enjoy life with us
while you are young and focus on your practice later, when you are old?" They tempted the Buddha this
way. However, when the Buddha pointed his finger at
the maidens, they immediately transformed into old
women. This transformation symbolically represents the
Buddha's realization that "pleasure is inherently linked to
suffering." In this metaphor, the young maidens symbolize pleasure, while the old women symbolize suffering.
While the meaning is profound, this imagery reflects the
worldview of ancient India and may not align well with
modern perspectives.

Another expression compares this temptation to a

"beautifully painted jar filled with excrement." This is also a symbolic expression. The well-painted jar represents joy, while the excrement symbolizes suffering. This analogy conveys the idea that pleasure and suffering are inherently linked. When we say, "Life is suffering," it is often misunderstood as pessimism, but that is not the intended meaning. The Buddha's teaching points to the truth that the very nature of joy contains the seeds of suffering. Pursuing desire brings temporary joy when it is fulfilled, but when it remains unsatisfied, suffering arises.

We try to eliminate suffering and hold onto joy, but in reality, this is impossible. Even when desire is fulfilled, it does not remain static. Desires grow, and when they are not met, suffering returns. Consequently, the pursuit of desire can never lead to complete or lasting happiness.

The Buddha realized, during his practice, that joy and suffering are inseparable as they are intrinsically connected. He understood that the root of suffering lies in desires and cravings, and thus, to be free from suffering, one must become free from desire. However, when one becomes free from desire and suffering ceases, joy also disappears along with it.

Foolish people seek joy and inevitably experience suffering. The wise, on the other hand, let go of joy in order to be free from suffering. For this reason, happiness for a practitioner is not defined as joy but rather as the absence of suffering—peace, serenity, and tranquility. This state is called "nirvana."

The temptation of Mara, as mentioned earlier, reflects the cycle of joy and suffering, which continually repeats itself. This is what is called reincarnation or "samsara," the cycle of birth and rebirth. In Indian traditional thought, reincarnation means being reborn as an animal or a human in another life after death. However, the reincarnation that the Buddha spoke of refers to the cycle of joy and suffering, indicating that joy is not sustainable since it inevitably turns into suffering. The Buddha called this cycle of joy and suffering "the suffering of reincarnation." To escape reincarnation means to reach a state without suffering which is called nirvana in Sanskrit and nibbana in Pali.

●

Overcoming Hatred and Anger Through Compassion

When the Buddha resisted the temptation of the maidens sent by Mara, it signified that he had transcended desires and greed. After failing to tempt the Buddha, Mara sent 10,000 soldiers to attack the Buddha with arrows, spears, and fire. How would we feel if someone attacked us? Naturally, we would become angry and upset. However, the Buddha responded with compassion and pity for his attackers. Then, the arrows aimed at him transformed into lotus flowers and fell to the ground. Mara's army was defeated by the Buddha's compassion. This scene symbolizes the complete eradication of deeply rooted anger, rage, hostility, hatred, and other negative emotions from the Buddha's heart.

Seeing that the Buddha had freed himself from needs, desires, hatred, and anger, Mara himself appeared before the Buddha and said, "Practitioner, if you give up your practice, I will give you my throne."

Mara offered the Buddha his own position, which can make all wishes come true so that the Desire Realm would not collapse. But the Buddha replied, "There is nothing I desire." Since desire is the foundation of the Desire Realm, the Buddha, having no desire, could not be tempted by Mara's offer.

Mara then tried a different tactic, saying, "Even if you practice with such diligence, you will never attain enlightenment or reach nirvana."

The Buddha replied, "You have earned your position through a single act of great merit, but I have accumulated infinite merit over many past lives. Therefore, I will attain enlightenment."

Hearing this, Mara, the king of Paranirmitavasavarti, said everyone knew he became a great king through the merit he accumulated and mocked the Buddha, saying that he doubted whether such a person with such a humble figure could have accumulated infinite merit. In response, the Buddha raised one hand from his meditation posture, touched the top of his head, stroked his knee, and then pointed to the ground, saying, "Earth goddess, bear witness to my past merit." At that moment, the earth goddess rose up from the ground and recounted the Buddha's innumerable past acts of merit, leaving Mara ashamed and defeated. Hearing her words, Mara retreated in shame.

On the night of the Buddha's enlightenment, he assumed a posture with his right hand pointing to the ground and his left hand resting in meditation, which is known as "the Earth-Touching Gesture," meaning "the hand gesture of pointing to the ground when receiving Mara's surrender."

●

The Law of Dependent Origination:
All Things in the World
Are Interconnected

After receiving Mara's surrender, the Buddha entered into deep meditation. As the morning star appeared, he finally attained enlightenment. Then, as a light dispelling the dark in the thick of the night, the Buddha realized the true nature of the world. How did he perceive the world before this realization? He saw it as a collection of countless independent and individual entities, appearing to compete with each other, engaging in the survival of the fittest and natural selection. However, after attaining enlightenment, the Buddha saw that all things in the world were interconnected and interdependent rather than independent and separate.

Let's use a hand as an example. If you cover the palm and look only at the five fingers, they might seem separate from one another. They differ in shape and function. However, once the palm is revealed, you can see that all five fingers are connected to form a single hand. Similarly, all things in this world, whether physical or mental, are not isolated, individual entities but are interconnected and interdependent. This is the teaching of dependent origination.

In the sutras, it is written that the Buddha realized the Law of Dependent Origination. Spatially, everything in this world is interconnected, while temporally, everything is impermanent and constantly changing. Causes lead to effects, and effects, in turn, have causes. The Buddha saw this spatial and temporal interconnectedness of all things, the true nature of the world.

After realizing the Law of Dependent Origination and understanding the true nature of the world, the Buddha was able to resolve all the questions he had since his youth. In the Indian caste system, it was believed that Brahmins and royals were distinct from commoners and slaves, but this was not true. In reality, everyone is interconnected rather than existing separately. If commoners didn't exist, nobility wouldn't exist either, and vice versa.

The Buddha taught that nobility and inferiority are not inherent qualities of existence, but we mistakenly make that distinction due the error in our perception. This realization was revolutionary for his time, as it challenged deeply ingrained social structures. With this understanding, there was no longer any reason to feel inferior due to a humble background, nor any justification for arrogance stemming from a noble background. The Buddha expressed this insight with the following verse:

Because this exists, that exists;
because this does not exist, that also does not exist.
Because this arises, that arises;
because this ceases, that also ceases.

From then on, the Buddha approached and conversed with everyone from the perspective of understanding, "What is the true nature of reality?" He did not teach or advocate his insights for personal gain or out of any bias or prejudice. Instead, his teachings were guided solely by the pursuit of truth and the benefit of all beings.

The Buddha's enlightenment was profoundly different from the yoga practices and meditation he had learned from his previous teachers. He realized that even a single leaf or a grain of sand beneath his feet was interconnected with him. This realization was the essence of the Buddha's great insight into the Law of Dependent Origination. Before, he had understood the world as a collection of countless independent parts like 20,000 separate components of a car placed in a basket. However, after his enlightenment, he saw the world as those parts assembled into a functioning vehicle—an interconnected whole. This is the Law of Dependent Origination.

Many of the questions we grapple with, such as "How should we view inequality and disharmony?" can be understood through the Buddha's teachings on Dependent Origination. The Middle Way, free from extremes, and the principle of Dependent Origination are two unique aspects of Buddhism, first revealed to the world by Gautama Buddha. These perspectives offer a distinct way of viewing and understanding reality, the true nature of things.

Chapter 03

THE BUDDHA BEGINS
TO SPREAD THE DHARMA
TO LIBERATE SENTIENT BEINGS

The Dhamek Stupa in Sarnath, Varanasi

01.
The First Turning of
the Wheel of Dharma

●

There Is No Effect
Without a Cause

Under the Bodhi tree, the Buddha real-
ized that all things in the world are interconnected and
interdependent. Everything in the world is not only
spatially related but also temporally connected through
cause and effect. Therefore, no effect occurs without a
cause, and if there is a cause, an effect will surely follow.
This is referred to as the Law of Causality.

The idea of "retributive justice" is popular in many
religions. Retributive justice is the concept of reward-
ing good and punishing evil, a system where evil deeds
are inevitably punished, and good deeds are inevitably
rewarded. This is a moral concept of reward and punish-

ment common in religion. However, the Law of Causality is like the laws of physics, where causes naturally lead to results. For example, let's say a person gets injured by a falling sign while walking on the street. People would view the event differently depending on whether they subscribe to the idea of retributive justice or the Law of Causality. Based on the concept of retributive justice, that person was inevitably injured due to past sins, God's punishment, or some other reason. In other words, it explains the event in terms of retribution.

However, the event would be described differently with the Law of Causality. It would explain that the person got injured because of certain causes and conditions, such as the timing of the person passing under the building, the strength of the wind, and the condition of the sign. Thus, retributive justice and Law of Causality offer completely different perspectives. Then, from the perspective of the Law of Causality, what should be done? First, the injured person should go to the hospital for medical treatment. Then, they should identify the cause of the accident. If a worn-out sign fell due to the wind, measures should be taken to inspect other signs to prevent future accidents. This is the perspective of the

Law of Causality, which differs from that of retributive justice.

Retributive justice is the perspective expressed by most religions. People believed that even if someone committed a bad deed and did not receive punishment immediately, they would eventually be punished by the heavens. They had the religious belief that if one was not punished in this life, they would be punished in the next. In contrast, the Law of Causality, based on the Law of Dependent Origination, is the law that explains how things change.

●

Those Who Have Closed Their Ears Cannot Hear the Dharma

The Buddha wished to share the Law of Dependent Origination with others. When he thought of who could understand it, the first people who came to mind were his two former teachers. The second group he thought of was his five friends, who had practiced with him for six years before leaving him. When those friends saw the Buddha stop his extreme ascetic practice, bathing in the river and eating the milk-rice pudding provided by Sujata after realizing the futility of asceticism, they became disappointed in the Buddha. They thought, "Gautama has abandoned his practice."

The five friends, who had practiced alongside the Buddha, criticized him and left. At the time of the Buddha's enlightenment, those friends were practicing 250 kilometers away in Sarnath, near Varanasi. The Buddha thought they would be the most likely to understand the Law of Dependent Origination and the Law of Causality that he had realized. So, the Buddha set out to find his friends.

The first people the Buddha met after attaining enlightenment were those he encountered on his way to meet his friends. During the journey, he had opportunities to teach the Dharma to several people. One day, five weeks after attaining enlightenment, he met a Brahmin. The Brahmin asked the Buddha, "What is true nobility?"

The Buddha replied, "Nobility is not determined by birth. It is achieved through a person's actions."

The Brahmin, however, could not accept the Buddha's teaching. Since the Buddha's words were contrary to what he believed, he dismissed the teaching and walked away. The Brahmin believed that nobility comes from birth, so when the Buddha said nobility is achieved through one's words and actions, the Brahmin scoffed and left.

In the seventh week, two merchants passing by made offerings to the Buddha. As they made offerings, they only prayed for the success of their business; they did not inquire about the Dharma. On another occasion, the Buddha met an ascetic who did ask about the Dharma, but when it did not align with his own views, he turned away. Also, when the Buddha reached the Ganges River, the ferryman refused to take him across because the Buddha did not pay the fare. The ferryman, preoccupied with making a living, had no ears to hear the Dharma.

The people the Buddha encountered on his journey reflect the attitudes of modern individuals. Whether in the past or present, people often become attached to noble status, positions of power, honor, or material blessings. Others are preoccupied with the struggles of daily life and cling to them. Some fixate on certain ideologies or beliefs. In doing so, they lose the precious eyes and ears needed to hear the teachings and perceive the truth. This phenomenon is not unique to the life of the Buddha. Similar examples can be found in the lives of Jesus,

Confucius, and other great sages throughout history.

●

Turning the Wheel of Dharma
for the First Time

The Buddha crossed the Ganges River
and went to Sarnath to find his five former companions.
When his friends saw him approaching from a distance,
they recognized him and said to one another, "Isn't that
Gautama coming over there? He abandoned his ascetic
practice. Why is he coming to us? When he arrives, let's
not treat him with the respect due a practitioner."

They agreed among themselves not to show him the
respect usually given to a practitioner, such as offering
water to wash his feet after a long journey and preparing a place for him to sit. However, as the Buddha
approached, they instinctively responded, one rising to
fetch water and another offering him a seat. This reaction was not necessarily due to the Buddha's greatness
but rather a reflection of the trust and respect he had
earned during their time together in the past.

As the Buddha sat down, his five friends said, "Gautama, you look well." This comment had a double

meaning. While this remark could be taken as a polite greeting, it also carried a hint of mockery, implying, "You gave up asceticism and started eating well; no wonder you look healthy."

In response, the Buddha replied, "Do not call me Gautama anymore." So, his friends asked the Buddha how they should address him, and the Buddha answered, "Call me Tathagata."

His friends found this hard to believe, because the word "Tathagata" means "thus come, thus gone," or "one who moves freely between reality and truth." In other words, it signifies someone who has fully realized the Law of Dependent Origination as the universal law. His friends continued to question the Buddha: "Are you saying you have attained enlightenment? How could you attain enlightenment after giving up your practice when you couldn't achieve it while practicing extreme asceticism in the past?"

As his friends showed disbelief, the Buddha said to them, "During the six years we were together, did I ever lie to you even once?" Hearing the Buddha's words, they quickly reconsidered and began to trust him. They asked the Buddha to share the teachings he had realized, and they prepared a place for the Buddha to teach the Dharma. The Buddha spent the early evening meditating with his companions, and in the middle of the night, he relaxed his meditation and adopted a calm and peaceful mindset. Then, the Buddha delivered his first Dharma talk at dawn.

When you are tense or excited, it becomes difficult to grasp the truth. To ensure that the teaching could be received without bias or preconceptions, he created an atmosphere of ease and openness, fostering a state where genuine dialogue could take place.

The Buddha explained to his friends, "Before I renounced the world, I pursued pleasure by following desires. For six years following my renunciation, I practiced asceticism and suppressed my desires. I realized that both of these lead toward one extreme. I attained enlightenment through the Middle Way of neither following nor suppressing desires, but merely recognizing desires as they are. You, too, must abandon extremes."

He then introduced the Four Noble Truths, explaining that by understanding the nature of a problem, identifying its cause, eliminating that cause, and thereby resolving the problem, one can achieve peace of mind.

Hearing the Dharma, one of his five friends, Kondanna, gained his "eyes of wisdom." From that point on, he was known as Anna Koṇḍanna, meaning "Kondanna who has realized the truth." Kondanna stood up and paid his respects to the Buddha as a teacher.

The Buddha, recognizing that Kondanna had attained enlightenment, declared with joy, "Kondanna has attained enlightenment. Kondanna has attained enlightenment!"

The Buddha rejoiced. However, the remaining four had not yet attained enlightenment and continued to listen to the Buddha's teachings. After three days, two of them attained enlightenment. After a week, his remaining two friends also attained enlightenment. At last, all five friends attained the eyes of wisdom. Filled with joy from the Buddha's teachings, they respectfully asked the Buddha to formally ordain them. Then, the Buddha said, "Come, bhikkhus! The Dharma has been well explained. Practice pure conduct and extinguish your suffering."

The Buddha's first Dharma talk that enlightened his five friends is called the "First Turning of the Wheel of Dharma." The Buddha thus gained five disciples, otherwise called the first disciples or the Five Bhikkhus. With the emergence of six arhats, the Three Jewels were complete. The Buddha became the Buddha Jewel, the teachings proclaimed in Sarnath became the Dharma Jewel, and the five bhikkhus became the Sangha Jewel.

●

Taking Refuge in the Buddha
After Hearing the Dharma

One day, while the Buddha and the five disciples were meditating peacefully, a young man passed through the forest on horseback. Seeing the young man, the Buddha said, "That young man will come here tomorrow morning and become a practitioner."

Upon hearing those words, the five bhikkhus responded, "Lord Buddha, that will not happen. That young man is Yasa, the only son of Kuriga, the wealthiest merchant in the kingdom. How could he ever become a monk?"

At that time, Yasa was riding a horse through the Sitavana charnel ground where the Buddha and the five bhikkhus were practicing. As he passed by with a frown on his face at the sight and smell of the rotting corpses, Yasa was surprised to see a practitioner sitting peacefully amidst the pile of corpses. That sight left a deep impression on him, and he passed by with his palms pressed together, a gesture of respect.

That night, Yasa hosted a grand banquet at his home. Yasa and his friends enjoyed themselves, drinking, dancing, and singing with dancers until they fell asleep in a drunken stupor. Yasa awoke early in the morning, and the flickering candlelight revealed the sight of his friends and the dancing women lying scattered around, drunk and asleep. The women who had been dancing with his friends were sleeping face down or on their sides. Some were sleeping with their legs over others' bodies. To Yasa, they resembled the entangled corpses he had seen the previous day in Sitavana. Overcome with anguish, Yasa fled from his home, exclaiming, "How did the once beautiful banquet hall turn into a Sitavana? Oh, how miserable I am! How miserable I am!"

Engulfed in despair, Yasa recalled the serene ascetic he had seen sitting calmly amidst the pile of corpses the previous day and went to the Sitavana. There, Yasa encountered the Buddha at dawn and poured out his sorrow. The Buddha invited him to sit and began teaching him the Dharma. Though Yasa had never practiced before and had previously lived a life of indulgence, he quickly grasped the teachings and attained awakening. How could this be possible? The banquet Yasa had enjoyed the previous night was full of pleasure. But the scene he saw at dawn resembled a pile of corpses. Since he had experienced this truth firsthand, he easily accepted the Buddha's teachings, just as a white cloth absorbs dye effortlessly.

Yasa, whose eyes of wisdom had opened, expressed his desire to renounce the world and be ordained on the spot. The Buddha accepted Yasa, saying, "Come, bhikkhu. The Dharma is well expounded here." At that time, the ordination process was not formalized. Like a light being lit in the dark night, he was awakened to the truth and realized the emptiness of all things in the world, thus becoming an ordained practitioner.

Meanwhile, at Yasa's home, his father, the wealthy merchant Kuriga, discovered his son was missing in the morning and had people search everywhere for him but to no avail. His friends, who had been with him the night before, reported that Yasa had disappeared by morning. Eventually, Kuriga found Yasa's shoes by the bank of the Varuna River, crossed the river, and met the Buddha. When he asked the Buddha if he had seen his son, the Buddha invited the merchant to sit for a moment and taught the Dharma, calming his worried mind. Once Kuriga was at ease, the Buddha called for

Yasa, and father and son were reunited.

Kuriga urged Yasa to return home, saying, "Your mother is heartbroken over your disappearance. Let's go home right away."

But Yasa refused, saying "I will follow the path of an ordained practitioner here."

His father protested, and told him to come home, saying, "No, you must come home. You were raised in wealth and cannot survive in the wilderness with its poisonous insects and wild beasts."

Yasa then asked his father, "Father, look at my face. Does it look more peaceful or more troubled than before?" Even to Kuriga, his son looked peaceful. Yasa continued, "Why should I leave this peaceful life to go back to a life of suffering?" As Yasa spoke about the peace of mind he had gained, his father, who had been worried about the practical matters of life like food, clothing, and shelter, found himself with nothing more to say.

Hearing that Yasa had found happiness through the Buddha's teachings, Kuriga asked the Buddha to teach him the Dharma as well. Upon hearing the Dharma from the Buddha, Kuriga also attained awakening. Overjoyed, Kuriga expressed his gratitude with the following verse:

"Great is the World-Honored One.

Great is the World-Honored One.

Like lifting up those who had fallen,

uncovering what had been covered,

showing the way to those who had been lost,

lighting up a lamp in the dark night,

you have awakened me

by teaching the Dharma using various analogies.

From now on,

I take refuge in the Buddha.

I take refuge in the Buddha's teachings.

I take refuge in the practitioners

who follow the Buddha's teachings."

Kuriga became the first lay disciple. He invited the Buddha to his house. The next day, the Buddha went to Kuriga's home with Bhikkhu Yasa, received a meal offering, and taught the Dharma to Yasa's mother and Yasa's wife. Both of them attained awakening through his teachings, and following Kuriga's example, the two also embarked on the path of lay practitioners. Now, there were male ordained practitioners, male lay practitioners, and female lay practitioners, forming the three groups of the assembly. Later, female monks also joined, completing the Fourfold Assembly of the Buddha's followers.

Yasa's four close friends found it hard to believe that he had renounced the world to become a practitioner. Just days ago, they had been indulging in pleasures together, and now Yasa's decision to pursue a life of a practitioner seemed absurd to them. They assumed that Yasa must have fallen under the influence of a strange person and decided to rescue him. When they went to find Yasa, they too were persuaded by him to meet the Buddha. After hearing the Dharma, they also became ordained practitioners.

Yasa, being the son of a wealthy merchant, had many friends across different regions. Hearing that Yasa had been "deceived," 50 friends from various kingdoms also came to "save" him. However, after being encouraged by Yasa to meet the Buddha and listen to his teachings, they too joined the Sangha.

Now there were a total of 61 arhats who had attained enlightenment: the five bhikkhus, Yasa and his four friends, the 50 friends who came later, and the Buddha. The Buddha declared, "There are 61 arhats, enlightened ones, in this world," and urged them to go forth and spread the Dharma for the benefit and happiness of all beings.

The Buddha's Declaration of Propagation is as follows:

"I have freed myself from the fetters of gods and men.
You too have attained liberation.
Now, go forth and spread the Dharma.
For the benefit and welfare of the people,
teach the Dharma with coherence
in the beginning, middle, and end."

After making this proclamation, the Buddha decided to go to Uruvela to teach the Dharma. This marked the beginning of his great journey to share his teachings with all beings. The story of the Buddha's enlightenment and teachings, as recorded in the sutras, continues to inspire people greatly to this day.

02.
Laying the Foundation for
Spreading the Dharma

●

Meeting Uruvela Kassapa

By teaching the Dharma, the Buddha opened the path of becoming ordained practitioners for Yasa and his friends. He also opened the way for Yasa's family to practice as lay followers. After the Declaration of Propagation, the Buddha encouraged all 60 ordained disciples to go their separate ways and spread the Dharma for the benefit of all people in the world. He himself returned alone to Uruvela, where he had once practiced asceticism for six years.

It was here in Uruvela that a significant event unfolded, one that would leave an indelible mark in the history of spreading the Dharma. Near the place where the Buddha had practiced asceticism, lived three brothers named

Kassapa, who were widely known and revered. Although the Buddha was largely unknown in the area, the Kassapa brothers had earned great fame. They led a religious sect that worshiped fire, and each had a large following of disciples. The eldest brother, Uruvela Kassapa, resided in Uruvela, while his younger brothers, Nadi Kassapa and Gaya Kassapa, lived in Nadi and Gaya, respectively. Together, they had over 1,000 disciples. The Kassapa brothers were so highly regarded that King Bimbisara of Magadha, the largest kingdom in India at the time, made offerings to them once a year. The Kassapas were treated with great respect and revered as spiritual teachers by the people of the kingdom.

The Buddha first went to the place where Uruvela Kassapa resided. Having practiced near the area for six years, the Buddha knew who Uruvela Kassapa was, but Kassapa did not know who Gautama Buddha was. It seems that Kassapa's community was somewhat closed. When the Buddha requested to stay the night, Kassapa refused, saying, "There is no space here for you to spend the night."

Despite the refusal, the Buddha asked again, saying any place would do. In many of the Buddha's conversion stories, expressions like "any place will do" or "any amount will do" appear frequently. This was like offering a blank check, which in Indian culture at the time was difficult to refuse. So, Kassapa could no longer decline and said, "There is no place for a person to stay, but if you insist, there is a snake pit where we keep the King Cobra."

This was meant as a refusal. However, the Buddha, undeterred, agreed to stay in the snake pit with the cobra. Uruvela Kassapa thought to himself, "This respected ascetic will likely be bitten and killed by the cobra." At that time, those who were devoted to asceticism were not very concerned with life and death. Moreover, Kassapa and his followers believed that since the Buddha had willingly chosen the dangerous snake pit, there was nothing they could do about it.

However, the next morning, the Buddha emerged from the snake pit as if he had slept peacefully. According to accounts, while the Buddha meditated, a cobra slithered out and coiled itself around him. Yet, due to the Buddha's calm and fearless demeanor, the cobra eventually uncoiled itself and quietly left. Seeing the Buddha come out unharmed, Uruvela Kassapa was impressed, yet he still held onto the arrogant thought, "He's remarkable, but he's not greater than me."

As a fire-worshiping ascetic, Uruvela Kassapa performed rituals involving fire. While the Buddha was with Uruvela Kassapa, one of Kassapa's disciples came running in a panic, saying that he had been trying to start a fire for a ritual but the fire would not ignite. Upon hearing this, the Buddha calmly said, "The fire is now lit."

The disciple had been trying to start the fire by rubbing wooden sticks together but had been unsuccessful. When the Buddha announced that the fire was lit, the disciple found it strange. However, upon checking, he discovered that the fire was indeed burning. Uruvela Kassapa grew suspicious, thinking, "Today, we are holding a large ritual with many attendees. I wonder what tricks this person will play?" He felt uneasy about the situation. To his relief, the Buddha was nowhere to be seen during the ritual.

After successfully completing the ritual that day, Uruvela Kassapa encountered the Buddha and said boastfully, "Where have you been? The ritual went very well today, and everything was in perfect order. It's a shame you didn't see it." The Buddha calmly replied, "Didn't you wish for me not to be present?"

Taken aback, Kassapa denied having such thoughts.

The Buddha then said, "You cannot attain liberation if jealousy lingers in your heart."

Upon hearing these words, Uruvela Kassapa suddenly became aware of his true feelings. During the time the Buddha stayed with him, Uruvela Kassapa had admired the young newcomer yet felt a sense of rivalry and jealousy. The Buddha, aware of these feelings, told him that in order to attain liberation, he must let go of jealousy. When Uruvela Kassapa recognized the competitiveness and jealousy in his heart, he felt peaceful. He knelt down and said to the Buddha, "I wish to become your disciple."

●

Extinguishing the Fire of the Three Poisons and Taking Refuge in the Buddha

Uruvela Kassapa, who had taken refuge in the Buddha, was an 80-year-old elder and a renowned leader with 500 disciples. Meanwhile, the Buddha was only 35 years old. The Buddha tried to dissuade Kassapa, saying, "I understand how you feel, but as a leader of 500 disciples, you should not make such a hasty decision. You have many disciples who depend on you."

At the Buddha's words, Uruvela Kassapa gathered his 500 disciples and declared, "Today, I have met a great teacher and attained a profound awakening. I intend to become his disciple, so you should all choose your own path." In response, his disciples expressed their wish to follow the same path as their teacher. The Buddha then gave a Dharma talk to Uruvela Kassapa's 500 disciples. After hearing the Buddha's teachings, their hearts opened, and they all decided to become ordained and become the Buddha's disciples. Then, they threw their fire-worshiping ritual tools into the river.

When the ritual tools floated downstream, Kassapa's younger brother, Nadi Kassapa, who was farther down the river, saw the sacred items drifting by and thought something terrible must have happened to his older brother. He quickly arrived with his 300 disciples to find his elder brother and his disciples, all with shaved heads, now ordained monks. Uruvela Kassapa urged his astonished younger brother to listen to the Buddha's Dharma talk. After hearing the teachings, Nadi Kassapa and his disciples also became the Buddha's disciples.

Kassapa's youngest brother, Gaya Kassapa, who lived farther downstream, saw the sacred items his brothers had cherished floating down the river. Overcome with fear, he hid in his place of practice, too afraid to come out. Therefore, Uruvela Kassapa personally brought the Buddha to where Gaya Kassapa was hiding and urged him to seek the Buddha's teachings. After hearing the Dharma, Gaya Kassapa and his 200 disciples also took refuge in the Buddha. In this way, all 1,000 fire-worshiping ascetics who heard the Buddha's teachings became his disciples.

The Buddha gave them the following Dharma talk:

"Until now, you have worshiped fire,
but now you have extinguished that fire.
However, the fires of greed, hatred, and ignorance
still burn within your hearts.
Extinguishing the flames of
these three poisons in your mind is
the true act of putting out fire."

This Dharma talk by the Buddha is called the Fire Sermon.

●

King Bimbisara's Heart Opens

The Buddha slowly proceeded with his 1,000 disciples toward Rajgir, the capital of the Kingdom of Magadha. They stayed at a place called Jethian, located about 15 kilometers west of Rajgir. News of the Buddha and his disciples quickly spread. King Bimbisara heard rumors that Uruvela Kassapa had met a young practitioner and had been ordained, but he could hardly believe it. A Brahmin priest and an ordained practitioner take different paths. Yet, his teacher, Uruvela Kassapa, a Brahmin, had become an ordained practitioner. That alone was astonishing, but the fact that he became the disciple of a young practitioner was even more unbelievable. So, King Bimbisara went out to meet them.

When he finally met Uruvela Kassapa and the Buddha, King Bimbisara said, "I have heard rumors that Uruvela Kassapa has become the disciple of a young practitioner. I can hardly believe it. It seems even more incredible than a three-year-old child calling an eighty-year-old man his grandson."

Upon hearing the king's words, Uruvela Kassapa stood up, circled the Buddha three times, put his palms together, and said, "This person is my teacher, and I am his disciple. Before meeting him, I planted the seeds of samsara. But after meeting him, I attained enlightenment and abandoned the seeds of samsara."

Only then did the king and ministers finally accept that the young man was indeed the Buddha and that Uruvela Kassapa had become his disciple. The phrase "planting the seeds of samsara" referred to the pursuit of blessings. In the past, they had worshiped "fire" and constantly sought blessings. However, even when one attains blessings, those blessings eventually run out, and the cycle of joy and suffering repeats. In the end, one cannot escape the cycle of reincarnation. However, Kassapa's enlightenment and his cessation of seeking blessings signified his declaration of liberation from reincarnation.

The king then requested the Buddha to teach him the Dharma. When the Buddha delivered the teachings, the king's heart opened. Overjoyed, the king said, "When I was a prince, I had five wishes: the first was that I would become king; the second, that the Buddha would appear in my kingdom; the third, that I would meet the Buddha in person; the fourth, that I would hear the Buddha's Dharma; and the fifth, that I would understand those teachings. Now all these wishes have been fulfilled." He then requested the Buddha to accept his offering of a meal at the royal palace.

●

Establishing Veluvana, the First Monastery

The Buddha declined King Bimbisara's offering, signifying that ordained practitioners do not accept hospitality in such luxurious places as the royal palace. In response, the king offered the bamboo grove outside the palace as a place for the Buddha and his disciples to stay and practice. This became the first monastery, Veluvana, also known as the Bamboo Grove Monastery, where practitioners following the Buddha's teachings gathered to practice. In those days, a "monastery" was not a building like the temples we know today, but a grove or forest where practitioners could dwell. This was a monumental event, as the Buddha had secured a place of practice for his disciples by converting a great religious leader and the ruler of the largest kingdom in India.

This was not the first encounter between the Buddha

and King Bimbisara. When the Buddha was practicing asceticism for six years, the king had seen a young practitioner walking with great dignity through the streets of Rajgir, and he had proposed that they rule the kingdom together. That young ascetic was Siddhartha Gautama from Kapilavastu. However, the Buddha had declined the proposal with the following words:

"Great King, I left my own kingdom, renouncing the throne, so why would I desire another kingdom? I abandoned my own country, so why would I take someone else's?"

At that time, the king had requested that if Siddhartha Gautama attained enlightenment, he should come back and guide him, and Siddhartha had promised to do so. True to his promise, the Buddha taught the Dharma to King Bimbisara.

●

Do Not Build Your Happiness on the Misfortune of Others

Three years after King Bimbisara took refuge in the Dharma, the Buddha went to the kingdom of Kosala at the invitation of a wealthy merchant named

Sudatta. At that time, Kosala was the second-largest kingdom in India after Magadha, and King Pasenadi of Kosala, having heard of the Buddha's reputation, came to meet him at Jetavana Monastery.

King Pasenadi asked, "I want to be a great king. How can I become a great king?" A typical response to such a question might be that a king needs a powerful army, a thriving economy, or divine favor. However, the Buddha's answer was different:

> "Love your people as you love your only son.
> Help the poor and comfort the lonely.
> Then, you will not need to practice asceticism.
> Do not build your happiness
> on the misfortune of others."

In those days, kings regarded the lives of their subjects as insignificant as the lives of flies. However, through the Buddha's famous teaching, "Do not build your happiness on the misfortune of others," King Pasenadi also became a disciple of the Buddha.

Today, much of our happiness is built on the misfortune of others. When we pass an exam, someone else fails. When we win an election, someone else loses. This aligns with the very questions that motivated the Buddha to renounce the world: "Why must one die for another to live? Why must one be unhappy for another to be happy?"

King Bimbisara of Magadha often engaged in philosophical discussions with the Buddha, while King Pasenadi of Kosala was known for asking more worldly questions. One story recounts a conversation between King Pasenadi and his wife. During their discussion, the king expressed his belief that he himself was the most precious thing in the world, even more valuable than wealth or the throne. Curious, he asked his wife what she considered most precious. She replied that she valued herself above all else.

In those days in India, it was unusual for a woman to make such a statement, as societal norms dictated that a husband was the most important person in a woman's life. Similarly, for subjects, the king was regarded as the most precious. Yet the queen boldly declared that she valued herself the most. To settle the matter, the king and queen sought the Buddha's opinion. The Buddha responded, "Yes, indeed, for each person, nothing is more precious than oneself."

As the Buddha said, the most precious thing in the

world is oneself. Yet today, we live our lives tormenting ourselves. Moreover, we become slaves to things that are not truly valuable—wealth, power, fame, and pleasure—wasting our precious lives.

Also, during the time that the Buddha was practicing with his disciples at the Veluvana Monastery, some of the greatest disciples who would play significant roles in the history of Buddhism came to join the Sangha after hearing about the Buddha. This included Sariputta, known for his wisdom, Moggallana, renowned for his supernatural powers, and Mahakassapa, the foremost in ascetic practice. They all took refuge in the Buddha after listening to his Dharma talks during this period. After instructing his 60 disciples, including the first five monks and Yasa's friends, to spread the Dharma, the Buddha also set out on his journey to teach and enlighten many people.

The Buddha taught the Dharma to Uruvela Kassapa and his disciples, who were great priests with significant spiritual influence over many people. He also converted the kings of the powerful kingdoms of Magadha and Kosala. In addition, as distinguished disciples heard the Dharma and took refuge in the Buddha, a solid foundation for spreading the Dharma was firmly established within five years after his enlightenment.

03.

The Ordination of
the Great Disciples

●

King Suddhodana Fails
to See the Buddha

Through his teachings, the Buddha enlightened many people, including influential figures like the religious leader Uruvela Kassapa and King Bimbisara of Magadha. Numerous people took refuge in the Buddha after hearing his Dharma talks. However, when one's mind is closed, even if they see and hear the same things as others, they are unable to truly see or hear. This was also true for the Buddha's father, King Suddhodana.

When King Bimbisara of Magadha invited the Buddha to his palace, the Buddha declined to enter. Likewise, when the Buddha returned to his homeland and his father, King Suddhodana, requested him to come to the palace, the Buddha refused. When King Suddhodana expressed his disappointment, the Buddha said, "This is the tradition of our family."

When King Suddhodana questioned where in the royal lineage of the Shakya tribe there was a tradition of asking for alms, the Buddha replied, "This is the tradition of ordained practitioners."

The Buddha had completely let go of the idea that he was royalty. Such tensions between the enlightened Buddha and his father, King Suddhodana, persisted. King Suddhodana frequently disapproved of the Buddha and his disciples wearing humble robes, sleeping under trees instead of in a proper lodging, and living on alms. King Suddhodana insisted that as a prince, the Buddha should not live like a beggar. He often asked questions like "Where does the Buddha sleep? What does he eat?" However, King Suddhodana never once asked what teachings the Buddha gave.

As a result, when the Buddha returned to his homeland, many young people of the Shakya tribe listened to his teachings and attained enlightenment, but King Suddhodana failed to attain enlightenment until the day he died.

The disciples found this situation difficult to understand and asked, "Even those of low caste, like the barber Upali, gain the eyes of wisdom by listening to the Dharma talks. Why, then, is King Suddhodana, the most distinguished among us, unable to open his eyes to the Dharma?"

In response, the Buddha explained, "In King Suddhodana's mind, there was only his son, not the Buddha."

King Suddhodana saw the Buddha solely as his son. He could not see his son as the enlightened Buddha.

●

Sariputta and Moggallana Become the Buddha's Disciples

The Buddha practiced with around 1,000 practitioners at the Veluvana Monastery, donated by King Bimbisara. It was possible for a community of 1,000 practitioners to sustain themselves by gathering alms each morning because Rajgir was a large city.

In the great city of Rajgir, there were many spiritual communities. Among them was a group that followed a teacher named Sanjaya. This group held a skeptical view, believing that "It is impossible to know the truth about anything." In some respects, their views were somewhat similar to the Buddha's teachings. Among Sanjaya's followers were two prominent disciples: one was Sariputta and the other was Moggallana.

One day, Sariputta saw one of the Buddha's disciples walking slowly in his alms round. He was very impressed by how the disciple walked with concentration, without getting distracted. This disciple was Assaji, the last of the first five disciples to attain enlightenment.

Sariputta followed Assaji and asked, "You look truly admirable. Who is your teacher and what does he teach?" Assaji replied, "I am a disciple of Gautama Buddha. However, I am not knowledgeable enough to explain his teachings to you. You should go and ask him yourself."

When Sariputta requested just a brief explanation, Assaji said, "All phenomena in this world have causes and effects. Where there is a cause, there will certainly be an effect. When a phenomenon occurs, there is always a cause. Like two sheaves of hay leaning against each other in a field, all existences in this world are interdependent."

Upon hearing Assaji's words, all of Sariputta's doubts were resolved. After finding out where the Buddha was staying, he returned to his place of practice. Moggallana, Sariputta's friend, noticed his brightened expression and asked if something good had happened. Sariputta then shared what he had heard from Assaji, and upon hearing this, Moggallana's own doubts were also cleared.

The two decided to seek out the Buddha and agreed that they should invite their teacher to join them. Sariputta went to their teacher, Sanjaya Belatthiputta, and told him about Assaji and the Buddha's teachings, inviting him to come along. However, being a skeptic, Sanjaya expressed doubts and refused to go. When the two set out to meet the Buddha without their teacher, 250 other practitioners in their group decided to join them. After listening to the Buddha's teachings, they all attained enlightenment and became ordained.

It is said the early disciples of the Buddha numbered 1,250. This number was reached when Sariputta, Moggallana, and the 250 practitioners who practiced with them became ordained. Since they practiced together at the Veluvana Monastery, they are often referred to as the 1,250 bhikkhus.

Sariputta and Moggallana were both older and had been practicing longer than the Buddha. Sariputta, in particular, was so wise that some people even mistook him for the Buddha. Uruvela Kassapa, Sariputta, and Moggallana were all from the Brahmin caste, the highest caste in India. In addition to being highly educated, their background as former Brahmin priests enabled them to play a major role in systematically organizing the Buddhist monastic order. Sariputta, especially, was instrumental in establishing the precepts and organizational structure of the Sangha, which is why he is known as the "foremost in wisdom."

On the other hand, Moggallana was already known for his exceptional supernatural powers before meeting the Buddha, which is why he is called "foremost in supernatural powers." At that time in India, possessing supernatural powers was considered a great skill. A religion defined by mysticism could gain followers and influence by displaying supernatural powers. However, the Buddha prohibited the use of supernatural powers because he believed they led people into ignorance and delusion. The Buddha taught that individuals should open their eyes of wisdom and take control of their own lives, but fascination with mysterious phenomena would likely lead them further into ignorance.

However, later on, some Buddhist factions began equating supernatural powers to one's level of practice, which contradicts the Buddha's teachings. The Buddha also prohibited fortune-telling, which includes practices like reading facial features, palmistry, astrology, or selecting auspicious dates. A practitioner should be free from fear, anxiety, and suffering in any situation; therefore, there is no reason to engage in fortune-telling. It is essential to recognize the differences between the Buddha's original teachings and certain aspects of modern Buddhism. We should aim to understand the Buddha's original teachings rather than just learning about Buddhism as a religion.

●

Mahakassapa Renounces Worldly Riches and Takes Refuge

Sariputta, foremost in wisdom, and Moggallana, foremost in supernatural powers, were both older and passed away before the Buddha. After the Buddha's passing, the Sangha was led by Mahakassapa. To avoid confusion with Uruvela Kassapa, he was called Mahakassapa, with "Maha" meaning "great."

Mahakassapa was also from the Brahmin caste, and

not only held a high social status but was also very wealthy. Despite his noble background and affluent upbringing, he had little interest in worldly matters, including marriage. However, when his parents persistently urged him to marry, he carved an exquisitely beautiful image of a woman from fragrant wood and presented it to his mother, saying, "If there exists a woman as beautiful as this, I will marry her."

Mahakassapa's intention was to avoid marriage. However, his mother traveled far and wide with the wooden figure, determined to find a woman who matched its beauty, and eventually, she succeeded. Mahakassapa, unable to go back on his word, had no choice but to marry.

On the first night of his marriage, Mahakassapa explained to his bride that he had no interest in worldly pursuits and had married solely to fulfill his parents' wishes. To his surprise, his wife revealed that she felt the same way—she, too, had been pressured into marriage by her parents. The two agreed to maintain the outward appearance of a married couple to honor their parents while they were alive. After their parents passed away, they decided to go their separate ways. Standing back-to-back, Mahakassapa and his wife parted ways, one setting out to the east, the other to the west.

After setting out on his journey, Mahakassapa went straight to the Buddha and asked to be ordained. Upon hearing Mahakassapa's request, the Buddha said, "Come, Mahakassapa; I have been waiting for you for a long time."

However, even after becoming a disciple of the Buddha and living as a practitioner, Mahakassapa seemed to have had difficulty shedding the habits of his wealthy upbringing. This was illustrated in a story involving his robe.

During the Buddha's time, there was no specific attire for ordained practitioners. Many practitioners wore "pamsukula" robes, garments made from cloth that had been used to cover corpses. Mahakassapa, having come straight from home, continued to wear the fine clothes he had arrived in.

One day, the Buddha said to Mahakassapa, "Venerable one, your robe is quite fine." Upon hearing this, Mahakassapa noticed that while the Buddha was wearing tattered robes, he himself was dressed in silk. So, Mahakassapa rose from his seat, took off his robe, and offered it to the Buddha. Then, he put on the Buddha's tattered robes.

After this incident, Mahakassapa lived an extremely frugal life. He only wore ragged clothes, did not accept meal invitations, only ate alms food, and always slept under trees. Therefore, Mahakassapa is known as the "foremost in ascetic practices." "Ascetic practices" refer to renouncing greed for material comforts—food, clothing, and shelter—and devoting oneself solely to practice.

With a single comment from the Buddha, Mahakassapa completely shed his old habits from his wealthy upbringing and adopted an even more frugal lifestyle than most. Practitioners of that time all led simple lives, but Mahakassapa's frugality was so extreme that there is an anecdote of other ordained practitioners looking down on him for being too shabby.

The story of Mahakassapa's robe carries symbolic meaning. In Buddhism, the act of passing on the Dharma to a disciple was often marked by the teacher presenting their own robe and alms bowl as a token of transmission. Mahakassapa inherited the Buddha's robe, signifying that he was the first disciple to inherit the Buddha's Dharma. The robe (kasaya) was made from cloth that had once covered corpses, and the alms bowl (baru) symbolized alms gathering, signifying that practitioners should live simply.

●

The Establishment of
Jetavana Monastery

It was around this time that the Buddha
met an important lay disciple, Sudatta. In Rajgir, there
was a wealthy merchant named Kalandaka who provided generous support to the Buddha and his disciples.
Kalandaka had a merchant friend named Sudatta who
conducted business in the city of Shravasti in Kosala
Kingdom. Whenever Sudatta came to Rajgir, he would
stay at Kalandaka's place, talking all night with his
friend, and when Kalandaka visited Shravasti, he would
stay at Sudatta's house, talking through the night and
having a good time with his good friend.

One day, when Sudatta arrived in Rajgir, he waited
for Kalandaka, who would usually come running out to
greet him, often without even taking the time to put on
his shoes. However, this time, Kalandaka did not appear
for a while, leaving Sudatta feeling slightly hurt.

When Kalandaka eventually came out, Sudatta asked,
"What has kept you so busy? Are you marrying off your
son or daughter?"

Kalandaka replied, "I wouldn't keep you waiting for

something like that."

Seeing Sudatta's puzzled expression, Kalandaka explained the reason for the delay. He shared that he had invited the Buddha and his disciples to his house for a meal the following day and had been busy preparing for the event. This was the first time Sudatta, who lived in Shravasti, had heard about the Buddha. As Kalandaka described the Buddha and his teachings, Sudatta became increasingly excited. The thought of meeting the Buddha filled him with such anticipation that he could hardly sleep that night.

The following morning, unable to sleep, Sudatta woke up early and went for a walk. Soon, he saw a practitioner sitting in the woods. At that moment, he realized this must be the Buddha whom Kalandaka had spoken about. Sudatta approached and asked, "Are you the Buddha?" The Buddha replied, "I have been waiting for you for a long time."

After hearing the Buddha's teachings, Sudatta was deeply moved, and he invited the Buddha to visit Shravasti. When the Buddha accepted the invitation with silence, Sudatta hurried back to Shravasti ahead of the Buddha to find a suitable location similar to the Veluvana Monastery in Rajgir. He eventually established

Jetavana Monastery outside of Shravasti and offered it to the Buddha and his disciples.

Jetavana Monastery is the place where the Buddha stayed the longest. The Buddha spent 45 years teaching the Dharma and observed a total of 45 retreats, 19 of which were spent at Jetavana Monastery, which means he stayed there for nearly half of his retreats. Consequently, many sutras, including the *Diamond Sutra*, are set against the backdrop of Jetavana Monastery. In the *Diamond Sutra*, Jetavana Monastery is referred to as "Jeta's Grove, Garden of Anathapindika." This name combines "Jeta's grove," referring to the forest of Prince Jeta, and "Anathapindika" (meaning "giver of alms to the lonely and destitute"), indicating the monastery built by Anathapindika, or Sudatta, and includes the origin of how Jetavana Monastery was established.

Sudatta was not only a successful businessman but also long dedicated to helping the poor. In India at the time, "poor" people referred to four groups: women without husbands, men without wives, children without parents or caretakers, and elderly people with no children to support them. A person who supported such people was called "Anathapindika." Thus, Anathapindika became Sudatta's nickname.

After meeting the Buddha and returning to Shravasti, Sudatta began searching for a suitable place to build a monastery like the Veluvana Monastery. He soon found an ideal location that was neither too far nor too close to Shravasti, accessible yet peaceful during the day and quiet at night, secluded enough to avoid distractions, and suitable for meditation. The location Sudatta found was Prince Jeta's grove. He went to the prince and asked him to sell the grove, but Prince Jeta firmly refused.

When Sudatta persistently requested to buy the land, offering to pay any price, Prince Jeta replied that he would sell the land if Sudatta covered it entirely with gold coins. However, Prince Jeta had no intention of selling the grove. Undeterred, Sudatta brought a cart loaded with gold coins and began laying them on the ground, but he was unable to cover even a small section of the entrance. Determined, Sudatta urged his servants to bring more gold coins from home. Seeing Sudatta's efforts, Prince Jeta said, "That is enough, Sudatta. You may stop. I will donate the remaining land as a gift. This will also be a blessing for me."

This is how Jetavana Monastery was established and how the phrase "Jeta's Grove, Garden of Anathapindika" mentioned in the *Diamond Sutra* came to be.

Chapter 04

EQUALITY,
the Right of
All Human Beings

The Ashokan Pillar in Vaishali

01.
Women Are
Half of the World

●

Allowing
Women to Be Ordained

The Buddha taught the Dharma on the road for 45 years, without discriminating based on social status, caste, or any other factor, so that all people could attain enlightenment.

In those days, societies worldwide were male-dominated, and India was not only male-centered but also rigidly caste-based. Kings of powerful nations, high priests, Brahmins, and wealthy merchants who met the Buddha took refuge in him after listening to his teachings. Then, how did the Buddha treat the lower caste people, who were discriminated against based on caste, and women, who were discriminated against based on gender?

At that time in India, women had no human rights whatsoever. Men, no matter how incompetent, held inheritance rights, while women, however accomplished, had no rights at all. Women were expected to serve men as their masters throughout their lives. As girls, they served their fathers, after marriage they served their husbands, and if their husbands died, they served their sons. This was known as the "three obediences," meaning that throughout her life, a woman would serve three different masters. At weddings, the father takes the daughter's hand and hands it over to the groom, right? While it may seem like a touching tradition, this act symbolized a change of ownership, which is not a positive cultural practice. Regardless of how it may appear, if we seek gender equality, we should consider changing such customs.

In the Buddha's time, lower caste people who performed heroic acts in war or made great contributions to the country could sometimes be selected by the king and be given an opportunity for upward social mobility. However, there are no records of women, even those born into noble families or as princesses, holding the same rights as men. This illustrates how very low the status of women was in Indian society at that time.

However, the Buddha recognized women's rights, which was not accepted in society at that time. We can see that the Buddha treated all people equally through the situation of the Shakya tribe after the Buddha's renunciation. After the Buddha renounced the world and King Suddhodana passed away, the Buddha's stepmother, Mahapajapati, found herself without a husband or son. Additionally, since the Buddha's younger brother and his son, Rahula, had also been ordained, Mahapajapati was left with no male relatives in her immediate family. The Buddha's wife, Yasodhara, was in a similar position. With both her husband and son ordained, she was left without her spouse and child.

Within the Shakya tribe, many households were left with only women as men left to become ordained. Many of these women had listened to the Buddha's teachings, attained awakening, and were living as lay practitioners. The women of the Shakya tribe, now free from familial ties with men, also wished to become ordained practitioners. Therefore, when the Buddha was staying in Kapilavastu, Mahapajapati and the other women requested the Buddha to allow women to be ordained. However, the Buddha did not grant this request. She asked once more, but again, the Buddha did not allow it.

Later, the Buddha left Kapilavastu and went to Vaish-ali. Yet, Mahapajapati and 500 other women, including Yasodhara, remained firm in their wish to be ordained. Determined, they followed the Buddha to Vaishali. There, they approached him again, requesting ordina-tion, but again the Buddha declined.

The Shakya women, who deeply longed to be or-dained, were heartbroken, and tears streamed down their faces. They had endured a long journey from Ka-pilavastu to Vaishali and looked exhausted and dishev-eled. With shaved heads in preparation for ordination, the 500 women's feet were swollen, their bodies covered in dust, and they could do nothing but weep. Ananda, the Buddha's attendant, witnessed this scene. As the Buddha's cousin and relative of Mahapajapati, Ananda's heart ached seeing the women in such distress.

Venerable Ananda went to the Buddha and asked, "If a woman renounces the world and practices diligently, can she attain enlightenment?" In response, the Buddha replied that women, too, could attain enlightenment if they practice diligently. Ananda then asked, "Then, why do you not allow women to be ordained?"

The Buddha told Ananda to say no more about it, but Ananda continued. He spoke about how much hardship

Mahapajapati, the Buddha's stepmother, had endured in raising the Buddha and of her immense merit. When the Buddha acknowledged the great merit of Mahapajapati, Ananda pleaded with him again, "Since Mahapajapati's merit is so great, please allow women to be ordained under your precepts and teachings."

At last, the Buddha consented, saying, "I permit women to be ordained."

This is how women were allowed to be ordained.

●

Letting Go of Dependency and Choosing the Path of Practice

After the Buddha began spreading the Dharma, the path for men to become ordained practitioners opened. Then, male and female lay practitioners emerged. Finally, the path for female ordained practitioners opened as well, about 20 years after the Buddha began spreading his teachings.

Why, then, did the Buddha delay allowing women to be ordained for so long, despite teaching that women were no different from men? By looking at the cultural and social context of the time, we can see why the Buddha initially could not allow it. At that time in India, women could not hold a name or identity independent of a man, and they could not become an independent person. Ordination meant that a woman would bear her own name and become an independent individual without the protection of a man. This was simply unacceptable in the culture and customs of the time.

Additionally, practitioners of that era renounced attachments to all things, lived in the forest, wore tattered clothes, and subsisted on alms, unhindered by anything. In those days, a woman without a man was considered open for anyone's taking; a woman sitting alone in the forest would almost certainly face harassment or assault. Therefore, recognizing women as ordained practitioners was impossible not only due to gender discrimination but also because of these safety concerns. This was why the Buddha initially did not allow women to be ordained. However, it is noteworthy that he permitted women's ordination in Vaishali, a progressive city at the time. Vaishali was the only republic in India, while other regions were absolute monarchies. A confederation of nobles governed Vaishali, giving it a democratic structure similar to that of Greece. It was also a society rich in resources, where various thinkers could coexist freely.

Therefore, while granting women an independent status was challenging in India, Vaishali, as the most open and progressive city, was a place where such a change could be attempted.

Another reason the Buddha allowed the ordination of Mahapajapati and the women who came with her was that they had let go of their dependence on men and demonstrated self-reliance and a resolute attitude. Since women were conditioned to depend on men, they developed a sense of dependency and subordination. Yet, "liberation" means letting go of dependency. For those who are deeply reliant, it is hard to abandon this habit. No matter how much they practice, it is difficult for them to let go of that habit. These women, however, undeterred by the Buddha's initial refusal, made the independent decision to travel to Vaishali. Though they were women, they had overcome dependency and subordination, showing determination in walking such a long way. This resolute spirit likely played a significant role in the Buddha's decision to allow women to be ordained. The Shakya women who followed the Buddha to Vaishali and demonstrated their own determination to take the path of a practitioner helped pave the way for the ordination of women.

●

The Buddha Recognizes
Women's Autonomy

The Buddha's decision to allow women to be ordained was a groundbreaking act at that time. Even today, in the 21st century, Catholic nuns are not permitted to become priests. Particularly in India, gender discrimination is even more severe than caste discrimination. So, the Buddha's decision to permit women's ordination 2,600 years ago was even more revolutionary than we might imagine.

The Buddha not only permitted the ordination of Mahapajapati and the women who came with her, but he also approved the ordination of courtesans, who were looked down upon by everyone. There was a courtesan named Uppalavanna. She became a courtesan out of revenge after being abandoned by both her first and second husbands and became the owner of a large brothel with 500 courtesans.

Hostile to the Buddha and his disciples, non-believers bribed Uppalavanna to try and tempt the Buddha. Uppalavanna approached the Buddha, accompanied by her 500 courtesans, and addressed him boldly: "They say you have the power to subdue all beings, but I have the power to subdue all men. All your disciples are said to be outstanding because they follow your teachings, but my disciples have extraordinary skill in mastering men."

The Buddha replied calmly: "Woman, you are consumed by revenge and taking vengeance on countless men. But you are only causing more women to suffer the same misfortunes as you. Hatred cannot drive out hatred."

Upon hearing his words, she realized how foolish her actions had been and asked the Buddha to ordain her. The Buddha's approval of her ordination was met with criticism not only from his disciples but also from the general public. However, the Buddha did not worry about such criticism and allowed the ordination of Uppalavanna and all 500 courtesans. News of this decision spread, bringing widespread condemnation of the Buddha, and his disciples found it difficult to receive alms wherever they went. However, the Buddha made no explanations and waited patiently, refusing to compromise with the world over what was untrue.

However, 500 years after the Buddha allowed women's ordination, during the Gupta dynasty, gender discrimination intensified, leading to the abolition of female ordination. As a result, countries following Theravada Buddhism still do not recognize female ordination. The reason given for this abolition was that when women were first accepted as ordained practitioners, the Buddha initially refused, but later allowed it only after Venerable Ananda earnestly pleaded on their behalf. They claimed that this was not truly the Buddha's will. To eliminate female ordination, they needed justification. If it were accepted that the Buddha himself had permitted female ordination from the start, they would have had no grounds to abolish it. Therefore, they may have left the records of the Buddha refusing to ordain women and Ananda imploring him to do so in the sutra in order to lay the ground for the abolishment of the bhikkhuni order.

Allowing women's ordination 2,600 years ago—something challenging for even today's people to accept—was impossible without the Buddha's enlightenment and decisiveness. Female ordination was reestablished with the emergence of Mahayana Buddhism. In Mahayana Buddhist countries like Korea and Taiwan, the bhikkhuni order has been maintained. While there is still discrimination between monks and nuns, the existence of the bhikkhuni order provides a level of equality compared to

Theravada Buddhism. In Theravada Buddhist countries like Myanmar, Thailand, and Sri Lanka, women can also practice, but they wear white robes and are not given the right to wear the kasaya robe (monastic robe). In that regard, there is a big difference between Theravada and Mahayana Buddhist traditions.

Though there is still much room for improvement, I believe that the ordination of women marked the beginning of women's liberation and gender equality. In particular, the fact that women could hold their own names, independently of men, was truly groundbreaking. Women, who had always been known as some man's daughter, wife, or mother, were finally able to have their own identity as bhikkhunis.

However, in the social circumstances of that time, women having their own names and existing independently was bound to have side effects. There were frequent incidents of women meditating in the forest wearing tattered robes being sexually harassed or even assaulted by men passing by.

In one such incident, a female practitioner was deep in meditation when a man approached her and tried to seduce her, saying "Your eyes are so beautiful." Hearing this, the female practitioner gouged out her own eyes, handed them to the man, saying, "If they are so beautiful, you may have them." Naturally, the man fled in terror. Women practitioners went to such lengths to continue their practice.

In another incident, a bhikkhuni was sexually assaulted. Even though she was forcibly assaulted, people gossiped, claiming that she had broken the precepts simply because there had been sexual contact. Imagine how unfair this must have felt to the bhikkhuni. She approached the Buddha and asked if this counted as breaking the precepts. After hearing the story, the Buddha addressed the assembly of bhikkhus: "This bhikkhuni has not broken the precepts. Do not speak of this matter any further." Thus, practicing as a bhikkhuni was fraught with challenges and obstacles.

As time passed, restrictions were put in place to address some of these issues, including a rule that bhikkhunis could not practice alone in the forest. Additionally, a system for ordination was established for bhikkhunis that was quite different from that for bhikkhus. Men under the age of twenty are known as samanera and can become bhikkhus once they reach twenty. However, women under twenty are called samaneris, and even after turning twenty, they do not immediately become bhikkhunis. Instead, they must spend two years as probationary bhikkhunis, known as sikkhamana, or "women in training." After these two years, they may become full bhikkhunis. Thus, while men have a two-step process (samanera, bhikkhu), women have a three-step process (samaneri, sikkhamana, bhikkhuni).

The bhikkhunis' quarters were set up near the bhikkus' quarters to deter outside intruders. At that time, only courtesans and bhikkhunis would bathe openly by the river. Courtesans were independent women with their own names with no male guardian and were easily accessible to men. Since bhikkhunis also bathed by the river, people mistakenly thought they were also courtesans, causing social issues. Thus, a rule was established requiring bhikkhunis to bathe with their clothes on. Although these restrictions were imposed only on women and may appear discriminatory by today's standards, they were intended as protective measures for bhikkhunis.

The Buddha may not have been able to solve gender discrimination in society at large, but within the monastic Sangha, he acknowledged women's autonomy and worked to overcome gender inequality. In later generations, some gender biases have reappeared within the monastic community, but it is incorrect to view this as a reflection of the Buddha's own stance.

Although women in ancient India were often seen as the property of others, ordination allowed women to become the masters of their own destinies. By declaring that there was no discrimination whatsoever between bhikkhus and bhikkhunis in taking refuge in the Dharma and following the path to liberation, the Buddha was a pioneer of women's liberation. With the recognition of bhikkhunis, the Buddhist order was completed, consisting of the fourfold assembly: bhikkhus (ordained male practitioners), bhikkhunis (ordained female practitioners), upasakas (lay male practitioners), and upasikas (lay female practitioners).

02.

Spreading the Dharma
with Equality and Compassion

●

A Caste Society Dominates
India

Although the Buddha was born as the son of a noble king in India, he did not turn a blind eye to the oppressed lower castes and sought to teach them the Dharma.

India was a rigid caste society at the time. At the top was the Brahmin priestly caste, followed by the warrior and royal caste known as the Kshatriya, then the Vaishya, a commoner caste engaged in production and economic activity, and finally, the lowest caste, the Sudras, who were enslaved laborers.

India remains a caste-based society, although today it is divided into upper, middle, and lower castes.

Approximately 15% of the population belongs to the upper caste, which includes the Brahmins, Kshatriyas, and Vaishyas. Brahmins make up around 3%, Kshatriyas about 5%, and Vaishyas around 7%. The middle caste corresponds to the laboring Sudra class, comprising about 65% of the population. The lowest caste, previously known as the "untouchables" or Dalits and currently referred to as Backward Classes (BCs) makes up around 20%. They are currently engaged in a caste liberation movement in India but face intense social resistance.

Among the lower castes, some occupations allow contact with higher castes, such as cooking, laundry, childcare, hairstyling, and dressing assistance. The Dalits, considered outside the caste system entirely, are prohibited from approaching or living with those of higher castes and are only allowed to live among themselves and work outdoors. The Dalits have faced extreme social discrimination and have held the most despised occupations. The barber Upali came from the barber caste, while Nidhi, responsible for cleaning human waste, was an untouchable. Those who raised pigs or cremated corpses were classified as untouchables and faced severe discrimination, often not even being treated as human.

Their social standing and occupation were often reflected in their names and surnames, passing down through generations.

●

Though Stained with Excrement, the Cloth Is Originally Clean

The Buddha did not discriminate against the untouchables, who were considered impure and avoided by others. Instead, he enlightened them by teaching them the Dharma. One notable example is the human waste collector, Nidhi. One day, while Nidhi was walking with two buckets of excrement slung over his shoulders, he encountered the Buddha and his disciples. At that time in India, there was a prejudice that contact with an untouchable would bring bad luck, to the extent that an untouchable could be killed for stepping on a Brahmin's shadow. Fearing he might cross paths with the Buddha's group, Nidhi quickly veered off onto a narrow forest path. The Buddha, seeing this from a distance, also went onto the forest path.

Relieved to have avoided the Buddha's entourage, Nidhi continued walking, eyes cast down, only to suddenly find himself face-to-face with the Buddha. Startled, he stumbled, causing the excrement to spill on both his clothing and the Buddha's robes. Frightened, Nidhi begged for forgiveness, fearing for his life.

The Buddha, however, gently took Nidhi's hand, helped him to his feet, and guided him to a nearby stream to wash.

After they had washed, the Buddha asked, "Your clothes became soiled, but what happened after washing them?"

"They became clean," Nidhi replied.

The Buddha said to Nidhi, "That is so. This cloth is not inherently dirty; it became soiled by the waste, and washing it made it clean again. In the same way, people are not born impure. Impurity only clings to us temporarily. If you wash away the impurities of your mind, you, too, will become clean."

Hearing this, Nidhi experienced a profound awakening. When he expressed his wish to be ordained, the Buddha said, "Come, bhikkhu!"

Although Nidhi was an untouchable, the Buddha accepted him into the Sangha without any discrimination. In ancient India, it was unthinkable for an untouchable and a Brahmin to live together in the same space. Yet, regardless of one's origins, ordination cleanses all impurities for those from a low caste, while the high status associated with Brahmins disappears upon ordination. This is due to the greatness of the Buddha's teachings. For this reason, all ordained bhikkhus lived together in the same space as fellow practitioners.

This led to significant criticism from those outside the practice community, with Brahmin monks, in particular, facing additional condemnation. People would say, "Noble-born men are associating with the impure." For this reason, Brahmin disciples of the Buddha were truly remarkable individuals. Lower caste individuals could shed their low status through ordination, while Brahmins, who enjoyed high social standing, willingly endured social criticism to join the Sangha. The fact that they lived together with other practitioners from all castes without regard for social status was only possible because they had let go of any sense of superiority.

Despite the Buddha's teachings, caste distinctions persist in places like Sri Lanka today, where Brahmin monks and lower caste monks belong to separate Sanghas and do not associate with each other. Consequently, high caste followers seek high caste monks, while low-caste followers go to low-caste monks.

Although the Buddha's teachings abolished caste distinctions, the reality shows how difficult it is to overcome deeply ingrained social customs. The Buddha's Dharma embraced the ordination of both women and lower castes. However, after the Buddha's passing, women's ordination was abolished, and although ordination is allowed for lower castes, Sanghas are now divided by caste. At first glance, Buddhism might seem to support caste or gender discrimination, but this goes against the Buddha's teachings.

The Buddha often said,

"In this world, there are four castes.
Yet within my Dharma, there is only one.
Just as there are four great rivers in the world
that merge into one upon reaching the ocean,
so too within my Dharma,
all are one."

In this way, 2,600 years ago, the Buddha broke down the barriers of caste and false beliefs through his teachings, achieving what could be called a "revolution." This was not a revolution of taking power through armed conflict but rather a mental and human rights revolu-

tion, a spiritual revolution that freed people from oppression.

●

No Class Discrimination
in the Buddha's Dharma

Another incident that demonstrates the
revolutionary caste liberation achieved through the Buddha's teachings occurred when the Buddha returned to
his hometown of Kapilavastu to teach the Shakya people. After listening to his teachings, many young people
decided to renounce the world. At that time, people had
to shave their heads themselves before ordination. So,
the princes of the Shakya tribe went to the barber Upali,
who usually trimmed their hair, and asked him to shave
their heads. Watching the princes abandon their great
wealth and high status to follow the Buddha, Upali, a
simple barber, thought, "I have nothing to give up, so
what am I clinging onto?" He, too, decided to become
ordained.

At this time, six years had passed since the Buddha
began teaching the Dharma, and Sariputta had already
established an orderly structure within the Sangha. Pre-

viously, those seeking ordination went directly to the Buddha, but now, the process required applicants to receive training and take vows from Sariputta. Unaware of this, Upali went straight to the Buddha to request ordination, and the Buddha immediately ordained him, as Upali had attained awakening after hearing the Dharma.

When the princes, who had resolved to become monks earlier, came to pay respects to the Buddha after completing their training under Sariputta, they lined up to bow before their elders. To their surprise, at the end of the line stood Upali, the very man who had once been their barber. Hesitating to bow before someone who had once been their servant, the princes wavered. Seeing this, the Buddha gently admonished them. In the sutra, there is a title that says, "There Is No Discrimination Within my Dharma. Bow to Upali," showing the Buddha's commitment to equality.

Another story further illustrates the Buddha's stance against discrimination. Among the Buddha's disciples, there was a man named Culapanthaka who was considered simple-minded. Unlike the other disciples, Culapanthaka found it very difficult to understand and practice the Buddha's teachings. The Buddha entrusted his talented disciples with teaching Culapanthaka, but they gave up, saying he was too dull to teach.

Thinking he couldn't stay in the Sangha any longer, Cudapanthaka prepared to return home in tears. Seeing this, the Buddha said to Cudapanthaka, "From now on, sweep the yard and clean the rooms while repeating, 'Remove the dust, wash away the dirt.'"

However, even these simple words were hard for Culapanthaka to remember. The Buddha then gathered his disciples and asked them to remind Culapanthaka to say, "Remove the dust, wash away the dirt" each time they saw him. This phrase means that our mind is inherently pure, but it is obscured by karma, similar to how dust or dirt accumulates. Just as we remove the dust and wash away the dirt, if we eliminate karma, we can find our innate Buddha nature.

As Culapanthaka heard this phrase repeated by the other disciples each time he cleaned, he diligently purified his mind, eventually attaining enlightenment and supernatural powers, becoming one of the sixteen arhats.

While these old stories might suggest that abandoning social status and humbling oneself is simple, the reality is quite different. True renunciation goes beyond simply deciding to "become a monk." It requires courageously letting go of fixed notions. Monastic life meant wearing discarded clothes, eating leftovers, and sleeping under trees, which required unwavering determination.

Even if people can imitate living as a practitioner after getting ordained, letting go of lifelong morals, social customs, and societal norms is far more challenging. The Buddha taught that these constructs are not the truth of existence but false beliefs created by humans. These false beliefs are what cause us to discriminate, create conflict, and live in suffering. Only by freeing ourselves from these constructs can we achieve true peace and a life free from fear. That is why the Buddha's stance against caste discrimination was so firm.

●

The Buddha Teaches the Dharma to Those Facing Hardship

There are many stories about the Buddha's compassion for the poor and those facing hardship. One story stands out for its insight. There was a young man who found practice extremely difficult. One day, he heard some Brahmins say that no matter how many sins a person has committed, they could all be washed away just by bathing in the Ganges River. That idea seemed so simple!

The young man went to the Buddha and asked, "The Brahmins say that no matter how many sins a person has committed, bathing in the Ganges River can cleanse them all and guarantee rebirth in heaven. Is this true?"

He found the claim hard to believe but was curious because so many people have believed it for too long. If it wasn't true, why would so many people continue to believe it? Hearing this, the Buddha smiled and said, "If what the Brahmins say is true, the fish living in the Ganges River would be the first to enter heaven." Hearing the Buddha's words, the young man attained enlightenment.

Here is another story. There was a woman named Kisa Gotami who was born into a poor family and endured a difficult life. A wealthy family promised to accept a bride of any social status as their son's wife if she could bear them a male heir. Kisa Gotami married into this family and eventually gave birth to a son. Her life transformed from one of discrimination and hardship to one of comfort and ease. However, her young son suddenly died.

As a mother, she was devastated by her son's death, but she also faced the terrifying prospect of losing her secure life. Her grief and fear were beyond words. With tears pouring down her face, she carried her dead son through the streets of Shravasti, pleading for someone to bring him back to life. But who could bring the dead back? Seeing her suffering, a compassionate person directed her to the Buddha at the Jetavana Monastery.

Believing the Buddha might revive her son, Kisa Gotami went to him and poured out her grief. The Buddha said, "Dear woman, go to Shravasti and bring me a handful of mustard seeds from a household where no one has ever died."

Kisa Gotami thought, "Perhaps the mustard seed is a miraculous medicine that will save my son." And gladly thinking she could obtain it, she went from house to house in Shravasti. At one house, she asked for a handful of mustard seeds and, upon receiving them, asked the owner, "Has anyone in this house ever died?"

The owner replied, "Yes, our grandmother passed away last year."

At the next house, she asked the same question and received the reply, "Yes, my father died three years ago."

Kisa Gotami had thought she could easily obtain the mustard seeds, but even after searching all day throughout Shravasti, she couldn't find a single house where no one had died.

Finally, she entered the last alley and came to the last house in Shravasti holding onto the last strand of hope. Kisa Gotami obtained a handful of mustard seeds and asked, "Has anyone ever died in this house?"

The owner exclaimed, "Where in the world would you find a house where no one has died?"

At that moment, Kisa Gotami attained awakening. Her sorrow disappeared, and she buried her son and returned to the Buddha.

The Buddha asked, "Did you bring the mustard seeds?"

Kisa Gotami replied, "Lord Buddha, I have no need of mustard seeds. I am now free from sorrow. Please guide me on the path to renunciation." Kisa Gotami, whose son had died, thus became an ordained practitioner.

The person described in the sutras as the most outstanding among female lay practitioners is Lady Visakha. She was born into a very wealthy family. She married into another prosperous family and became a generous supporter of the Sangha.

One rainy day, she came to the Buddha with tears streaming down her face. "What has happened? Why are you so sorrowful?" the Buddha asked.

Through her tears, Lady Visakha replied, "Lord Buddha, I am deeply saddened today. My most beloved granddaughter passed away this morning, and I cannot bear this sadness."

The Buddha, looking at Lady Visakha's face, suddenly asked, "Do you think it is better to have many loved ones or only a few?"

Hearing Visakha's answer that it was good to have many, the Buddha asked again, "Then, how would it be if someone had as many loved ones as the number of citizens in the city of Shravasti?"

Lady Visakha answered, "Lord Buddha, that person would be the happiest person in this world."

The Buddha then asked, "Lady Visakha, how many people do you think die each day in Shravasti?"

Lady Visakha replied, "Many people die. Perhaps around ten each day. At the very least, two or three people must die daily."

The Buddha said, "Lady Visakha, then the happiest person in this world would be crying in sorrow every day."

The moment she heard these words, Lady Visakha attained awakening. Though her tears still flowed, her face brightened as she said, "Lord Buddha, I understand."

When the Buddha asked his question, Lady Visakha replied that the happiest person in the world would be someone with as many loved ones as the number of citizens in Shravasti. However, this supposedly happy person would also experience the sadness of losing two or three loved ones every day. The idea that "the happiest person is also the saddest" is a paradox. The Buddha didn't offer words of comfort but instead provided a teaching to enlighten her. By realizing the truth that happiness and unhappiness are not intrinsically tied to the death of her beloved granddaughter, Lady Visakha overcame her grief and found inner peace. When we attain enlightenment, while we may still temporarily get caught up in sadness or suffering, we can free ourselves from suffering in any situation and achieve lasting peace of mind.

From these examples, we see that the Buddha treated the poor, the lower castes, and women with great compassion. In contrast, he rebuked and criticized kings and Brahmins who perpetuated caste and gender discrimination.

The Buddha approached the lower castes and women, who were persecuted and marginalized in society, without discrimination. Rather than presenting them with ideologically complex teachings, he awakened them by teaching the Dharma in a way that was easy for them to understand and resonated with their experiences. Just as a doctor prescribes medicine according to the patient's illness, the Buddha tailored his teachings to suit the circumstances of his audience. This approach is known as "tailored teaching" ("daegi seolbeop" in Korean).

Inspired by the Buddha, who tailored his teachings to guide sentient beings toward enlightenment, I conduct Dharma Q&As, aiming to lead people toward enlightenment by addressing their struggles in a manner that aligns with modern sensibilities. The Buddha accepted people's circumstances as they were but guided them to awaken from the ignorance of their own minds. In doing so, he opened the path to peace and happiness. This is the essence of his compassionate teaching.

03.
Steps Toward Peace

●

Human Blood is More Precious Than River Water

During the time of the Buddha, there were about 300 kingdoms with varying sizes in India, of which 16 were major powers. Among them, the two superpowers were the Kingdoms of Magadha and the Kingdom of Kosala. Much like the Warring States period in ancient China, this political landscape was rife with conflict and wars, prompting the Buddha to speak extensively about peace.

With the region fragmented into over 300 kingdoms, larger kingdoms often invaded smaller ones, and the smaller kingdoms resisted, leading to battles. Even smaller kingdoms sometimes fought among themselves.

Between Kapilavastu of the Shakya tribe and Devdaha of the Koliya tribe flowed a small river called the Rohini River. The two kingdoms shared a border along the river and typically enjoyed friendly relations, including frequent mutual visits and intermarriages between the two tribes.

However, one year, during a particularly severe drought, water scarcity led to tensions between the farmers of the two kingdoms who used the river for irrigation. The Shakyas thought that if they shared the river water with the Koliyas, the harvest on both sides would be ruined. Believing that their harvest would be saved if they diverted all the water to their side, the Shakya farmers told the Koliya farmers, "If we share the river water, the crop on both sides will fail, so we will use all the water." Hearing this, the Koliyas retorted, "If that's your position, we will also divert the water to our side so that we can use it."

What began as a verbal dispute escalated into fistfights. As farmers were already on edge due to the water shortage, fistfights between a few individuals quickly became full-blown brawls between the two sides. Later, the brawls grew to the point where people were throwing rocks and injuring each other. With the situation worsening, both kingdoms sent armies to protect their people. What began as a fight over water had spiraled into the brink of war between the two kingdoms.

The Buddha, foreseeing that if the situation were left unchecked, it would escalate into a large-scale battle involving arrows, swords, and spears, resulting in the deaths of many people on both sides, went to the site of the conflict. He summoned the generals from both sides. Since the Buddha's mother was from the Koliya tribe and his father was from the Shakya tribe, he was well-acquainted with both sides.

The Buddha asked the two generals, "Which is more precious, human blood or the water flowing in that river?"

Both generals responded the same way: "Lord Buddha, how can blood be compared to river water? Blood is infinitely more precious."

Then, the Buddha said to the two generals, "If you wage war over insignificant river water, will you not spill precious human blood as if it were mere water?"

At the Buddha's words, the agitated generals calmed down and realized their foolishness. They said to the Buddha, "We were wrong."

It is recorded that with the Buddha's guidance, both

sides stepped back from the brink of war and engaged in dialogue. They decided to collaborate on constructing irrigation channels and shared the river water, enabling them to endure the drought that year.

Today, when people discuss peace, the Buddha's intervention during the Rohini River dispute is one of the most frequently cited examples. The Buddha's message remains profoundly relevant:

"Let us live happily,
without hatred amidst hatred,
without conflict amidst conflict.
Let us live happily,
without illness amidst illness.
Let us live happily."

●

Persuading People Toward Peace Through Dialogue

The Kingdom of Kapilavastu, established by the Shakya tribe, was technically a vassal state of the larger Kingdom of Kosala. After the Buddha renounced worldly life, the throne of Kapilavastu was succeeded by his cousin, King Mahanama.

Among India's two great powers at the time, one was the Kingdom of Kosala, whose capital, Shravasti, was home to the Jetavana Monastery, where the Buddha spent much of his time. King Pasenadi of Kosala, already a devoted disciple of the Buddha, had several wives but deeply revered the Buddha and wished to marry a princess from the Shakya tribe.

The Shakyas, though from a smaller nation, were proud and independent-minded. They found it highly offensive that the powerful King of Kosala, who already had many wives, sought to marry one of their princesses. Considering it disgraceful to send a Shakya princess as a concubine to Kosala, they dressed up a beautiful maidservant as a princess and sent her instead. This maidservant bore King Pasenadi a son, Prince Virudhaka.

Since King Pasenadi had many concubines, there were also many princes in Kosala. These princes often visited their maternal relatives. However, as Prince Virudhaka's mother was originally a maidservant from Kapilavastu, she never visited her homeland. The young prince, however, begged to visit his maternal family like the other princes. Eventually, at the age of seven, he visited Kapilavastu for the first time.

The Shakyas treated the young prince with great hospitality, recognizing him as a prince from a powerful nation. He stayed there for several days and set out to return, but he remembered he left something behind and went back to retrieve the item. In the room where he had stayed, he overheard maidservants calling the place tainted and spraying salt everywhere to clean the room.

When Virudhaka returned and asked his mother why this had happened, his mother revealed the truth about her origins. From then on, Virudhaka harbored a great hatred toward the Shakya tribe.

When Virudhaka grew older, he staged a coup, overthrowing his father and ascending to the throne of Kosala. As king, he set out to attack Kapilavastu to take revenge. On his way, he saw the Buddha meditating under the scorching sun. Virudhaka dismounted his horse and asked the Buddha, "World-Honored One, why do you meditate under the scorching sun when there is a cool shade under that banyan tree?" The Buddha replied, "Great King, there is no shade better than the shade of one's own kin."

Moved by these words, King Virudhaka turned his army back. However, a few days later, his anger toward the Shakyas flared again, and he set out with his army once more. Again, he encountered the Buddha at the same spot. Once more, the Buddha's presence persuaded the king to retreat. This happened a total of three times, with the Buddha singlehandedly halting the army through peaceful dialogue. However, unable to quell his resentment, Virudhaka set out to attack once more, determined to go through with the invasion even if the Buddha appeared again.

This time, the Buddha was nowhere to be seen, and finally, King Virudhaka invaded Kapilavastu, the hometown of the Buddha. He ordered his soldiers to kill every male Shakya. Still, some escaped and dispersed across India and are said to be living as various castes today.

Although Virudhaka, after becoming king, invaded the Shakyas by force, the Buddha did not resort to violence to prevent the attack. Instead, he engaged the king in dialogue, attempting to resolve the conflict peacefully. Though his efforts did not ultimately prevent the invasion, the Buddha remained committed to peaceful resolution through persuasion and dialogue until the very end.

This approach to peaceful resolution can still be observed in modern times. For instance, when the South Korean government sought to designate the area around

Bongamsa Temple as a national park, most monks planned to oppose it through protests and rallies. However, Ven. Seoham Sunim opposed such measures, instead choosing to meet with the president at the Blue House. He reasoned that while nature must be protected, the culture of practice and the practice sanctuaries of practitioners were also worth preserving. Through calm and reasoned dialogue, Ven. Seoham Sunim successfully convinced the president to abandon the national park plan, resolving the matter peacefully.

Ven. Seoam Sunim believed that solving problems through the power of the masses is undesirable as it is still employing force to resolve a situation. Regardless of whether this method is right or wrong, we can see that it is important to do our best to resolve issues peacefully through dialogue and persuasion as much as possible.

●

Defining the Standards of a Great Nation

Even in his final year at the age of 80, the year he entered parinirvana, the Buddha emphasized resolving conflicts peacefully through rational compromise and dialogue.

At the time the Buddha was staying at Vulture Peak (Gijjhakuta) outside Rajgir, the capital of the Magadha Kingdom, Prince Ajatasattu staged a coup, overthrowing his father, King Bimbisara, to seize the throne. During this era, it was not uncommon for sons to kill their fathers or brothers to claim power. After becoming king, Ajatasattu prepared for war to invade the neighboring Vajji tribe. Wishing to consult the wise Buddha before initiating the war, the king sent a messenger to him. The messenger conveyed the king's greetings and posed the question:

"His Majesty, the King, is planning to invade the neighboring Vajjī tribe and wishes to know your opinion."

The Buddha did not answer directly but instead called upon Ananda and engaged in a dialogue with him.

"Ananda, long ago, the Vajji people asked me how they could govern their nation well and ensure its safety. I told them seven principles to follow. First, I advised them to gather frequently to discuss important matters. Do they still adhere to this principle?"

Ananda replied, "Yes, they still follow the advice."

Then, the Buddha asked, "Second, I told them to work in unity once they reach a decision based on frequent discussions. Do they still uphold this principle?"

Ananda affirmed, "Yes, they continue to follow it."

The Buddha continued, "Third, I advised them not to abolish established laws carelessly and not to create new laws unnecessarily. How are they doing in this regard?"

Ananda answered, "They respect the laws and do not change them recklessly."

The Buddha asked again, "Fourth, do they protect women and the vulnerable members of their society?"

Ananda confirmed, "Yes, they do."

The Buddha then inquired, "Fifth, do they honor the elderly, respect their experience, and heed their wisdom?"

Ananda again responded affirmatively, "Yes, they do."

"Sixth, do they preserve the customs, traditions, and lands handed down from their ancestors?" asked the Buddha.

When Ananda confirmed this as well, the Buddha asked one final question:

"Seventh, I advised that if there are wise individuals, even from other nations, they should be invited to share their opinions. Are they still practicing this?"

Ananda replied that they were, indeed, still adhering to this advice.

The Buddha then concluded, "If they are following these principles, their nation will prosper and neither fall nor decline."

Hearing this dialogue between the Buddha and Ananda, the minister of Magadha, who was present, said as he prepared to return to Magadha:

"World-Honored One, I understand now. If they are adhering to even one of these principles, it would be difficult for us to conquer them. But since they are following all seven, victory in war would be nearly impossible. I will convey this to the king and advise him to seek other ways."

The introductory portion of *Nirvana Sutra* (*Mahaparinibbana Sutta*), which records the Buddha's final journey, describes how, after the minister departed, the Buddha gathered his disciples at the Veluvana Monastery to teach them the seven principles that prevent the decline of kingdoms, in order to prevent the decline of the Sangha and the Buddhist order.

The first of the seven principles the Buddha mentioned that prevent a kingdom's decline is to meet frequently for discussions. In today's terms, this can be likened to democracy. Of course, achieving this is not easy when political parties, ideologies, or religions hold opposing views. Nevertheless, the Buddha's advice underscores the importance of convening and deliberating regularly, especially in challenging times.

The next principle is cooperation and unity. Even if people gather frequently to discuss issues before making a decision, it is often difficult for people to unite when their opinions are not fully reflected. A common weakness of democratic systems is the lack of cohesion. The Buddha taught that after resolving differing opinions through discussion and reaching a conclusion, it is essential to unite and work together. That is how strength is consolidated.

In today's world, even when there are differences of opinion during competition, the loser should congratulate the winner, and the winner should embrace the loser. Only through such cooperation can a nation move forward together. The Buddha's teachings on unity and collaboration remain highly relevant today and offer valuable lessons for our society.

The Buddha emphasized that laws should not be changed frequently. Unless there is a compelling reason, maintaining established laws is essential to preserve people's respect for and adherence to the legal system. Additionally, he stressed the importance of caring for the socially vulnerable, valuing the wisdom and experiences of elders, and preserving and passing down traditional culture.

Lastly, the Buddha highlighted the importance of listening to the views of practitioners or thinkers. Leaders should seek their insights to envision a better future. For instance, King Ajatasattu consulted the Buddha about war, and as a result, the Buddha was able to prevent a war that could have led to unnecessary sacrifice and failure. Respecting and listening to the advice of enlightened individuals is crucial. The Buddha's teachings on the seven principles for preventing a nation's decline remain relevant and practical even today.

In ancient India, conflicts were often resolved through brute force. However, the Buddha consistently guided people to resolve conflicts through dialogue and rational discussions rather than by force. Of course, the Buddha only provided guidance. If people did not accept it, there was nothing he could do. Some, like King Ajatasattu, embraced his teachings, while others, like King Viruḍhaka, rejected them. Ultimately, the choice to accept the Buddha's message of peace lies with each individual.

●

Forgiveness of Past Wrongs to
Those Who Truly Repent

There was a man named Angulimala who believed that the moment he put on a necklace made of a hundred human fingers, he could be reborn in heaven. "Anguli" means finger and "mala" means prayer beads. This horrifying practice led him to kill 99 people, and he was searching for his final victim to complete the necklace.

One day, the Buddha walked alone into the forest where Angulimala resided. Seeing him, Angulimala shouted, "Stop, monk!" and began chasing the Buddha. Yet, the Buddha continued walking calmly as if nothing were happening. When Angulimala caught up to him, blocking his path and preparing to strike with his sword, he demanded, "Why do you not stop when I tell you to stop?"

The Buddha looked at him and replied, "My friend, I have long since stopped."

Angulimala was confused and asked, "What do you mean? You kept walking and yet claim you have stopped. What are you talking about?"

The Buddha explained, "I have long stopped all arguments, judgments, and discriminations in my mind. Concepts of right and wrong, coming and going have ceased. But you, my friend, have yet to stop."

Upon hearing the Buddha's words, Angulimala was struck with a profound realization and repented before the Buddha. Listening to the Buddha's teachings, his mind was awakened, and he requested to be ordained. The Buddha accepted his request and gave him a new name, "Ahimsa," which means "non-violence."

After Angulimala was ordained, the public refused to offer alms and directed intense criticism toward the Sangha for accepting him. Eventually, Angulimala was struck by stones thrown by angry people and lost his life. However, he passed away without regret, resentment, or hatred.

04.

Not Wavering in the Face of Criticism and Slander

●

If You Don't Accept It, Criticism Remains with the One Who Gave It

Even someone as noble as the Buddha was criticized by others. Historical records show that many people denounced the Buddha. How did the Buddha respond to those who insulted, criticized, and sought to harm him?

One story illustrates the Buddha's response to personal insults. The Buddha once went to a Brahmin's house to receive alms. The Brahmin insulted him, saying,"Why does a healthy man like you live off others instead of working to earn your own living?"

The Buddha listened quietly and then asked the Brahmin, "Do you sometimes have guests at your house?"

The Brahmin replied, "Yes, I do."

The Buddha asked again, "Do they bring gifts when they come?"

The Brahmin answered, "Yes, they do."

Then the Buddha asked, "But if you don't accept their gifts, to whom do they belong?"

The Brahmin, irritated, replied, "Of course, the gifts still belong to the one who brought them."

The Buddha smiled gently, which further angered the Brahmin, who demanded to know why he was smiling.

The Buddha explained, "You've just offered me the gift of your insults, but if I don't accept them, to whom do they belong?"

Hearing those words, the Brahmin had a profound awakening and said respectfully, "Lord Buddha, I was wrong. Please come inside."

The Brahmin then offered the Buddha a meal, and after listening to the Buddha's teachings, he became a lay practitioner.

If we only consider the outcome—the Brahmin offering a meal, listening to the Buddha's teachings, and taking refuge in him—we might say this was a truly auspicious encounter. We might also believe that a good karmic bond from a past life led to their meeting in this life, and that their relationship will continue to be good in future lives.

But if it were someone like me instead of the Buddha, what might have happened when insulted by the Brahmin? I might have responded, "If you don't want to give me food, just say so. Why are you insulting me?

The Brahmin might have replied, "It's because you came to my house in the morning to beg for food."

In response to that, I might have retorted, "When did I ask you for food? I was just standing here."

Then, the Brahmin might have raised his voice even more, "Why are you standing in front of my house?"

And then I would likely have replied again, fueling the argument further, "Can't I even stand here?"

People observing the quarrel between us might have thought, "Look at those two, arguing as soon as they met. They must have had a bad relationship in their past lives. They're bound to meet again in this life and the next as enemies."

In this way, we often judge past and future lives based on present circumstances. If we respond to criticism with criticism, the karmic bond of animosity will persist for three lifetimes. However, if we respond to criticism with a smile, not only does the present improve, but also the past and future lives. That's why there is a saying, "A single smile can dissolve the karma of the past, present, and future."

Yet, smiling even once can be difficult. If we can smile, especially when someone insults, criticizes, or gets angry at us, we can become a Buddha. But it's nearly impossible to respond with a smile when someone insults us. It's much easier to want to fight back to the very end even if it means going to hell.

As we see in the Buddha's example, the other person has their own reasons for getting angry and insulting us. In such situations, offering them a smile could change the dynamic. Wouldn't it be worth trying?

●

Even in Silence, the True Dharma Dispels False Accusations

The Buddha's response to collective criticism offers insight into the attitude we should adopt in our own lives. This particular incident occurred when the Buddha was staying at the Veluvana Monastery after teaching the Dharma to King Bimbisara of Magadha.

Sariputta and Moggallana left their religious sect along with 250 of their disciples to take refuge in the Buddha after listening to the Buddha's teachings. The leader of that sect was furious and began spreading malicious rumors about the Buddha:

"Yesterday, he took someone's son. Today, he took someone's husband. Whose disciple will he take tomorrow?"

When someone was ordained under the Buddha, it often meant, from a parent's perspective, losing a son; from a wife's perspective, losing a husband; or from a teacher's perspective, losing a disciple. Exploiting this sentiment, the sect spread false rumors that the Buddha was "stealing" people, which turned public opinion against him.

As a result, the Buddha's disciples often failed to receive offerings when they went to collect alms in villages. The disciples shared their difficulties with the Buddha, explaining how the false rumors had made it challenging to receive alms.

The Buddha advised them, "When people say such things, respond by saying this: 'The Tathagata teaches the true Dharma. Who would not follow the true Dharma after hearing it?'"

The disciples conveyed the Buddha's words to the villagers. Within a week, the rumors and criticisms subsided. Listening to the disciples, the villagers began to change their views:

"The Buddha speaks only the truth. Whoever encounters this truth, whether it be someone's husband, son, or disciple, how could they not take refuge in the Buddha's teachings?"

At that time, in Shravasti, the capital city of Kosala Kingdom, there was a growing religious sect led by Nigantha Nataputta. In addition to Buddhism, there were six other prominent ascetic movements, collectively referred to in Buddhism as the Six Heretical Teachers. This was a time when various ideologies were flourishing. Besides the six ascetic groups, there were 62 groups with differing views, and in a broader sense, there were 360 different views altogether, reminiscent of the Hundred Schools of Thought during China's Warring States Period. With so many doctrines and claims, disagreements were rife, leading to intense debates. Each school tried to assert its superiority while denouncing others, creating a climate of significant intellectual and ideological conflict.

In the midst of this turmoil, the king took refuge in the Dharma after hearing the Buddha's teachings. Many people from other emerging sects also became the Buddha's disciples, and a growing number of lay people began to sponsor the Sangha. As more and more people took refuge in the Buddha and supported his teachings, rival sects grew envious and sought to damage the Buddha's reputation. They sent people to challenge the Buddha in debates, attempting to assert their dominance. However, they found it exceedingly difficult to refute the Buddha's teachings. Eventually, no one dared to challenge him anymore.

Frustrated by their failures, one sect devised a scheme to harm the Buddha's reputation using a beautiful woman. They selected the most attractive woman among their members' families and instructed her to walk toward Jetavana Monastery, where the Buddha was residing, every evening and return early in the morning.

When villagers noticed the beautiful woman walking late at night, they asked, "Where are you going at this hour?"

She would reply dismissively, "What business is it of yours where I go?"

The next morning, when villagers saw her returning from the direction of the monastery, they asked, "Why are you coming from that direction so early in the morning?

As instructed, she would respond, "It's none of your business."

This continued for some time, and suspicions began to grow among the villagers. Then, the rival sect instructed someone to murder the woman and hide her body beneath bushes in a nearby forest.

After the woman's disappearance, members of the sect pretended to search for her. The villagers recalled seeing the woman walking at night toward Jetavana Monastery, where the Buddha was staying, and coming from that direction in the morning. They shared this with the people from the sect. The sect then spread rumors that the Buddha and his disciples might have harmed the woman.

The rumor was very convincing, and the people of Shravasti searched the nearby forest and found the woman's body there. The rival sect carried the body through the streets of Shravasti, shouting, "Gautama Buddha's disciples did this heinous crime. Gautama may appear dignified on the outside, but he committed this despicable act."

As public opinion turned against them, the Buddha's disciples could no longer receive alms in the villages. It was indeed a major crisis. Yet, the Buddha advised his disciples not to respond to the villagers' accusations but instead to wait patiently. He instructed them to say the following regarding the rumors:

"Only they can know the truth. The one who committed the act knows the facts."

Initially, the villagers did not believe the disciples' words and retorted, "Exactly! Since you did it, of course, you would know the truth!"

However, not long after, the person who had killed the woman under the sect's orders got drunk and confessed to the crime. The truth of the incident came to light, and it was revealed that the scheme had been orchestrated by the sect led by Nigantha Nataputta. As a result, the reputation of the Buddha and his disciples grew even greater.

There had been another incident earlier where someone tried to defame the Buddha in a similar fashion. While the Buddha was giving a Dharma talk to the lay people, a woman with a swollen belly pushed her way through the crowd and interrupted his talk, saying,

"Ascetic, you give such good Dharma talk in front of others, but why don't you take proper care of me? In my womb is your child, so you should take care of me and the child. If not, shouldn't you tell your wealthiest disciple, Sudatta, or the king of this kingdom to provide for us?"

The crowd began murmuring at her accusations.

The Buddha, calm as ever, addressed the woman,

"Woman, you know the truth of this matter better than anyone else."

Hearing the Buddha's words, the woman replied, "Yes, of course, I know the truth best."

As soon as the woman finished speaking, a sudden gust of wind blew her skirt, revealing that she had placed a gourd under her clothes to appear pregnant. The woman had fabricated the story in an attempt to discredit the Buddha. Exposed and disgraced, the woman was dragged away.

These records of the Buddha's life demonstrate not only the intense ideological conflicts of that era but also the many attempts to defame and criticize the Buddha. Despite such baseless accusations, the Buddha remained unshaken by unjust slander and criticism, revealing his innocence with equanimity.

●

Embracing Jealousy and Criticism
with Compassion

The Buddha resolved violence and criticism stemming from jealousy through dialogue. Among the Buddha's disciples was a highly regarded disciple named Devadatta, a member of the Shakya tribe. As the Buddha aged, Devadatta made a proposal:

"How about I succeed you as the second Buddha and lead the Sangha after you?"

The Buddha replied to Devadatta,"The Sangha is not led by any one person. There is no need for someone to replace the Buddha. Practitioners should guide their own lives and be the masters of their own lives, so it is unnecessary to appoint a single leader."

Hearing this, Devadatta felt offended. He believed himself highly capable, possessing supernatural powers and giving excellent Dharma talks. Additionally, Prince Ajatasattu, even before ascending to the throne, had revered Devadatta as his teacher, providing him with generous offerings. Consequently, many of the Buddha's disciples followed Devadatta. However, the Buddha expressed concern about Devadatta receiving such lavish offerings from the prince.

One day, in front of the assembly, Devadatta said to the Buddha, "Lord Buddha, I have a suggestion." The Buddha granted him permission to speak. Devadatta then proposed three restrictions related to eating:

"A practitioner should collect alms. They should not accept invitations for meals. They should eat only one meal a day and abstain from eating fish or similar foods."

He also proposed restrictions regarding clothing and shelter:

"Practitioners must wear pamsukula, robes made from discarded cloth used to wrap corpses. They should sleep under trees or in caves and must not sleep under the eaves of houses."

Devadatta was expressing what he thought practitioners should rightly do. The Buddha agreed to all five of Devadatta's proposals.

"Very well. What you have suggested is reasonable. Let everyone follow these practices."

Devadatta's intention behind these proposals was to gain the Buddha's approval and, in doing so, establish himself as the Buddha's de facto successor. However, while accepting his suggestions, the Buddha added, "It is truly admirable for a practitioner to live that way. But Devadatta, while collecting alms is a good practice for a practitioner, it is also acceptable to occasionally accept meal invitations from devoted lay followers. While it is a good practice to eat one meal a day, it is permissible for the sick or young practitioners in their growth phase to eat two meals a day. Avoiding fish and adhering to a vegetarian diet is commendable, but when collecting alms, if the meal includes fish, one should accept it and not discard it. Wearing pamsukula robes is a noble practice. But if such robes are unavailable, a practitioner can wear new ones. Living under trees or in caves is truly admirable, but during harsh weather, such as on rainy days, it is acceptable to sleep under the eaves of abandoned houses."

The Buddha's additions to Devadatta's suggestions were universally reasonable and wise. No matter how virtuous a practice may be, it cannot always be strictly mandated. Circumstances and situations may necessitate flexibility and exceptions.

Devadatta, deeply disappointed that his intentions had not been realized, devised a plan to harm the Buddha. He hired someone to kill the Buddha, believing it would be an easy task since the Buddha often meditated alone in the forest. However, when the hired man approached the Buddha in deep meditation, he felt an overwhelming sense of unease and fear, preventing him from carrying out the act. He ended up dropping the weapon he was holding.

The Buddha called the man to come nearer and asked what had happened. The man answered truthfully, "I was hired by someone to harm you, but I was overcome with fear and anxiety that I could not possibly carry out the deed."

Hearing this, the Buddha said, "In that case, quickly take the back route to escape. If you go back down, those waiting in the forest may kill you to eliminate any evidence of their scheme." Upon hearing the Buddha's words, he quickly fled the scene.

Stories like this reveal the intense jealousy, criticism, and even attempts to harm the Buddha from both within and outside the Sangha. Yet, the Buddha remained unshaken, always maintaining his composure.

"The Tathagata knows no fear."

This statement reflects the Buddha's ability to face hostility and violence with unwavering compassion and equanimity.

When we are criticized or attacked by others, we unconsciously become defensive. However, the Buddha was not afraid of criticism from others and embraced even his adversaries with compassion. We should also learn from the Buddha's approach and work to resolve conflicts peacefully. Regardless of the situation, we should remain calm, avoid reacting impulsively, and refrain from overreacting to criticism.

Chapter 05

WHEN YOU MEET THE BUDDHA,
YOU ARE THE BUDDHA

The Parinirvana Temple and the Parinirvana Stupa in Kushinagar

01.
Freedom from
Old Age, Sickness, and Death:
The Path to Nirvana

●

Embarking on the Final Journey,
the Path to Nirvana

The Buddha renounced the world at the age of 29, practiced asceticism for six years, and attained enlightenment at the age of 35. For 45 years thereafter, he tirelessly taught the Dharma and guided the people without taking a single day of rest until he entered parinirvana at the age of 80. Let's explore the Buddha's final journey, the path to nirvana.

The Buddha's last journey began at Rajgir, Vulture Peak (Gijjhakuta), where he taught King Ajatasattu the "Seven Principles That Prevent the Decline of a Nation," thereby preventing a military invasion. After that, at Veluvana Monastery, he taught the "Seven Principles That

Prevent the Decline of the Sangha." Then, he passed through Ambalatthika Park, Nalanda, Pataliputra, and crossed the Ganges River to reach Vaishali.

At Vaishali, the Buddha rested under a mango tree. This mango orchard belonged to a famous courtesan named Ambapali. "Amba" means "mango" in Pali, a name given to her because she was abandoned under a mango tree as a child. Ambapali grew up to be so extraordinarily beautiful that many men vied for her hand in marriage. As a solution, the kingdom declared her a courtesan, making her available to all men instead of being married to just one. At that time, Ambapali was famous throughout the region, regarded as the queen of social circles.

Ambapali was so renowned that kings and wealthy merchants from various regions sought her company, offering to spend a night with her. She is said to have operated a large brothel with 500 courtesans under her care, reflecting her immense fame and influence.

In those days, it was customary for people to pay respects and make offerings to practitioners sitting under their mango trees. When Ambapali heard that the Buddha was in her mango grove, she hurried over in her chariot, greeted the Buddha, and requested a Dharma teaching. After hearing the Buddha's teachings, Ambapali attained awakening. Filled with joy, Ambapali said to the Buddha, "I would like to invite you and your disciples to my home for a meal tomorrow morning."

The Buddha silently accepted her invitation, and Ambapali quickly returned home in her chariot to prepare a meal for a large gathering the following day.

Meanwhile, members of the local royal family had also heard that the Buddha was in the area. Dressed in splendid attire, they rode in their chariots to pay their respects to him. On the way, they encountered Ambapali, who was rushing home. In her haste, the wheels of her chariot splashed mud onto the royals' clothes. Since they were both royalty and patrons of Ambapali, she had committed a grave offense as a courtesan.

The royals spoke angrily, "What urgent matter do you have that you are rushing like that without caution in our presence?"

Ambapali bowed her head in apology and explained, "Respected nobles, I apologize. I was in haste as I have invited the Buddha for a meal offering tomorrow morning. Please forgive me."

Hearing this, the royals were displeased, as they found it difficult to accept that someone of low status as Ambapali would offer alms to the Buddha before they could. After discussing among themselves, they said to her, "You invited the Buddha first? Then, give us the right to offer the meal instead."

At that time, it was socially expected that Ambapali would yield her invitation to the royals. However, she refused. The royals then offered her 1,000 gold coins in exchange for the opportunity, but Ambapali stood firm, replying, "Even if you offered me the entire city of Vaishali, I would not yield this opportunity."

Ambapali, once a woman who earned her living through singing and dancing, had grown confident and resolute after hearing the Buddha's teachings and attaining awakening. She left after proclaiming she would not yield even for 1,000 gold coins or the entire city of Vaishali.

When the royals arrived at their destination, they paid their respects to the Buddha and invited him for a meal the next morning. However, the Buddha refused, saying he had a prior engagement. In a society where women were not even considered equals, and courtesans were regarded with even less respect, the Buddha's decision to honor his commitment to Ambapali over the royals was extraordinary. This decision reflected the Buddha's belief in the inherent equality of all people.

Soon, the Buddha arrived in Vaishali. That year, the region experienced a famine, making it difficult for the Sangha to stay together in one place and practice. The Buddha instructed his disciples to disperse and spend the rainy season retreat separately. He himself spent the retreat in Beluva Village, accompanied by Ananda. During the retreat, the Buddha became gravely ill, and Ananda became deeply worried, fearing the Buddha might pass away. However, since the Buddha had left no instructions for his disciples about his passing, Ananda reassured himself that the Buddha would not leave them yet.

Meanwhile, the Buddha, reflecting on his condition, thought, "If I were to enter nirvana here, while my disciples are scattered during the rainy season, it would cause them difficulty." To extend his life for the benefit of his disciples, the Buddha practiced renewal of life energy and regained some strength. At the end of the retreat, he gathered his disciples and declared, "In three months, I will enter nirvana."

Then, like an elephant slowly turning to look back, the Buddha gazed back at Vaishali and said, "This will be the last time I see Vaishali."

The Buddha headed north. The people of Vaishali, hearing it was their last chance to see him, could not contain their sorrow and kept following him. Even as the Buddha crossed the Gandaki River, people remained on the riverbank, watching from afar, unable to bring themselves to leave.

To bid them farewell, the Buddha floated his alms bowl down the river as a parting gesture. In memory of the Buddha, the people later built a stupa using his alms bowl as a relic.

●

The Last Meal:
Receiving Cunda's Offering

The Buddha continued north and reached the village of Pava. There, he sat under a mango tree owned by a man named Cunda, the son of a blacksmith. Blacksmiths were low-caste manual laborers. Like Upali the barber mentioned earlier, Cunda also belonged to the lowest Sudra caste.

When Cunda heard that practitioners were sitting under his mango tree, he went to greet them and requested a Dharma teaching from the Buddha. After listening to the Buddha's teachings, Cunda attained awakening. Filled with immense joy, Cunda requested the Buddha, "Lord Buddha, I would like to offer a meal to you and your disciples tomorrow morning." The Buddha silently accepted Cunda's invitation.

After Cunda left, Ananda said to the Buddha with a worried expression, "Lord Buddha, Cunda does not have the means to prepare a large meal. Why did you accept his invitation?" The Buddha replied to Ananda, "He will prepare it well. Do not worry."

The next morning, Cunda indeed successfully prepared the meal. That year, the drought had been so severe that even the Buddha had not received a communal meal invitation since the one from Ambapali. There were times when the Buddha and his disciples went on alms rounds and could only obtain rice bran, typically used as animal feed. That was why Ananda had worried how Cunda, who was not wealthy, could possibly prepare a meal for a large group of people. Yet, Cunda had managed to prepare the meal.

During the meal, the members of the Sangha typically sit in a circle while the host serves the food into everyone's alms bowl. After serving several dishes, it was time to serve the last dish. The name of this dish was Sukara-maddava. After this food was served into the Buddha's bowl, the Buddha said to Cunda, "Cunda, this dish is difficult for ordinary people to digest. Do not serve it to the disciples. Instead, bury it in the ground."

After the meal, the Buddha gave a Dharma teaching to express gratitude to Cunda for his offering. However, after completing the teaching, the Buddha appeared to be in pain as he rose from his seat and said to Ananda, "Ananda, let us depart quickly. I am experiencing severe pain in my stomach."

As they traveled, the Buddha suffered from diarrhea, passing blood—a clear sign of acute food poisoning. At the Kakuttha River, he took his final bath, and after sitting down to rest, he asked Ananda, "How is Cunda doing?"

Ananda replied, "Cunda is deeply worried. He has been following behind the group, crying continuously. Everyone is saying that although Cunda made an offering to the Buddha, he gained no merit. They are blaming Cunda, saying that the Buddha might pass away after eating the food he offered."

The Buddha said to Ananda, "Bring Cunda here."

The Buddha had Cunda sit beside him and asked Ananda, "What is the offering that brings the greatest merit in this world?"

Ananda answered, "An offering made to the Buddha."

The Buddha said to Ananda, "Among the offerings made to the Buddha, there are two that bring the greatest merit. One is the last offering made before the Buddha attains perfect enlightenment. The other is the last offering made before the Buddha enters nirvana."

The offering made before enlightenment refers to the meal provided by Sujata, while the final offering refers to the meal taken before the Buddha's passing. Through the Buddha's words to Ananda, Cunda went from being perceived as the person who "caused the Buddha's death" to being honored as the one who made the final offering to the Buddha.

As a result, Cunda became recognized as a benefactor with merit, equal to that of Sujata. The worry and anxiety on Cunda's face disappeared, and the doubts within the hearts of the disciples were completely resolved.

We may eat poisonous food and either vomit, survive without harm, or avoid eating it altogether if we know in advance. But can we forgive the person who served us that food if it leads to our death?

The Buddha, however, encouraged Cunda by proclaiming that his offering carried the greatest merit in the world. In doing so, Cunda was recognized as the one who made the final offering to the Buddha, and later generations built a large stupa to commemorate it.

This exemplifies the Buddha's compassion.

●

Teaching the Noble Eightfold Path to Subhadda

The Buddha, dragging his ailing body, continued northward with his disciples and eventually arrived at Kushinagar. There, he entered a forest of sal trees. Between two sal trees, he laid down and said to Ananda, "This evening, I will enter nirvana. Go to the village and tell anyone who wishes to see me for the last time to come now."

Although it was not the flowering season, the sal trees began to bloom. When people marveled at this, the Buddha said,

"This is the final offering from the heavenly beings
to the Tathagata's nirvana.
However, Ananda,
this is not the highest offering.

The highest offering to the Tathagata is
to practice diligently according to
the Tathagata's teachings."

The Buddha explained that practicing diligently to
achieve a state free of suffering is the highest offering
one can make to him. The merit of such practice far sur-
passes any mysterious natural phenomena.

Ananda, concerned about the Buddha entering nirvana in the forest, asked,"Lord Buddha, why do you
choose to enter nirvana in this forest? Would it not be
more appropriate to do so in the palace of the Malla
kings here in Kushinagar?"

The Buddha replied, "Ananda, do not say such things.
If I enter nirvana in the palace, there will be people who
wish to see me but cannot enter. Here in this forest, anyone, regardless of caste or status, can come to see me if
they so desire." The Buddha always treated people equally, showing no discrimination.

Ananda went to the village and informed the people,
"The Tathagata will enter nirvana tonight. Anyone wishing to pay their respects should come now."

The villagers came in great numbers to bid farewell to
the Buddha. Despite organizing the visits by family, it

took until late into the night for everyone to finish their farewells.

As Ananda was hoping for the Buddha, who was resting, to enter nirvana peacefully, an elderly man arrived. The man, named Subhadda, a 120-year-old practitioner from another religious sect, came leaning on a staff. Subhadda insisted on seeing the Buddha, leading to an argument with Ananda.

"I must meet Gautama now," said Subhadda. Although Ananda said it was not possible at the moment, Subhadda kept insisting on meeting the Buddha, saying, "I have a question, and I heard that the Great Ascetic will enter nirvana today. If I do not ask now, I will never have another chance!"

Hearing their argument, the Buddha said, "Ananda, that person has not come to bother me but to ask a question. Let him in."

As soon as Subhadda saw the Buddha, who was lying down, he began asking questions in an argumentative tone, "There are many teachers in this world, each claiming their teachings are correct and those of others are wrong. Who among them is right, and who is wrong? Or are they all wrong? If you know the truth, please tell me."

The Buddha replied, "Subhadda, if there is greed, hatred, and ignorance in the heart, it is difficult to trust anything that is said. It is useless to talk about the words they have spoken. I will tell you the truth."

Follow the Noble Eightfold Path. First, have the Right View. See things as they are. Second, have the Right Thought. Understand that if there is a cause, there is an effect, and if there is an effect, there must be a cause. Third, use the Right Speech. Speak truthfully and kindly. Fourth, take the Right Action. Behave ethically and morally. Fifth, have the Right Livelihood. Earn your living in an honorable way. Sixth, engage in the Right Effort. Practice diligently. Seventh, maintain Right Mindfulness. Be constantly aware of the state of your mind. Eighth, have Right Concentration. Maintain tranquility and concentrate your mind on a single point."

Subhadda, who had always been preoccupied with debates about which teachings were right or wrong, realized the futility of such concerns and attained awakening through the Buddha's teaching.

Subhadda requested ordination from the Buddha, saying he wished to become his disciple. The Buddha replied, "Subhadda, our rule is that those from other sects must live with us for three months before we allow them to ordain. This is to ensure they are suited to practicing in the Sangha." Subhadda responded, "Even if you tell me to wait three years instead of three months, I will gladly do so." Hearing Subhadda's response, the Buddha allowed his ordination. Thus, Subhadda became the Buddha's final disciple.

●

Giving the Final Teaching to His Disciples

After the Buddha announced that he would enter nirvana that night, Ananda went to the nearby village to inform the people about the Buddha's passing. When Ananda returned, he felt a deep sense of emptiness at the thought of losing the Buddha and asked several questions.

"What should we rely on?" asked Ananda.

The Buddha replied, "Rely on the Four Establishments of Mindfulness: contemplation of the body as impure, contemplation of feelings as suffering, contemplation of the mind as impermanent, and contemplation of phenomena as non-self."

Ananda asked again, "What should we think about?"

The Buddha replied, "Think about the Four Sacred Sites: Lumbini, Bodh Gaya, Sarnath, and Kushinagar."

Ananda asked further, "Who should we take as our teacher?"

The Buddha answered, "Take my teachings and the precepts as your teacher."

Finally, Ananda asked, "We have gained great merit by making offerings to you, Lord Buddha. When you enter nirvana, to whom should we make our offerings?"

The Buddha replied, "Ananda, do not worry. There are four ways to make offerings that generate merit equal to offerings made to the Buddha. First, give food to the hungry. Second, give medicine to the sick and help them heal. Third, help and comfort the poor and the lonely. Fourth, protect those who practice with a pure heart."

This final conversation between the Buddha and Ananda is considered the Buddha's last instructions. They are reminiscent of the words of Jesus in the Bible. What did Jesus say was the criterion for entering heaven? He asked if one had fed the hungry, given drink to the thirsty, clothed the naked, healed the sick, visited the imprisoned, and welcomed the stranger, saying, "Whatever you did for one of the least of these brothers and sisters of mine, you did for me."

The teachings of sages have many similarities. Offering food to the hungry, treating the sick, and helping the poor are considered acts equivalent to offerings to the Buddha. Extending help to the "least of these" is a path to salvation. What matters is not what religion we follow but whether we practice according to the teachings of the Buddha or Jesus.

The Buddha consoled Ananda by saying, "Ananda, the Tathagata is not the physical body but the wisdom of enlightenment. Though the body will leave you, the wisdom of enlightenment will remain with you forever."

The Buddha then addressed his disciples one last time:

"If there is anything you wish to ask, ask now. After I have entered nirvana, regretting that you did not ask will be of no use. Ask now."

None of the disciples asked a question. Seeing this, Buddha spoke again, "Ask as a friend would ask another friend." Still, there was no response from the disciples.

Ananda then said, "Lord Buddha, we have no doubts. You have already taught us the Dharma, and we believe in and understand your teachings."

Hearing this, the Buddha said his final words:

"All conditioned things are impermanent.

Practice diligently,

like the constant dripping of

water penetrating a stone."

With these words, the Buddha peacefully entered nirvana.

When we reflect on the description of the Buddha's
passing, we can see that his behavior was unlike that
of an ordinary person confronting death. The Buddha
continued his daily life until his final breath, showing no
fear of death. When one has no fear of death, there is no
need to discuss where one goes after death.

What happened after the Buddha's passing? Before
the Buddha entered nirvana, when Ananda asked how
the funeral should be conducted, the Buddha replied,
"Ananda, do not worry about the funeral. Practitioners
need not concern themselves with such matters. The lay
people will follow their own customs."

The Buddha's instruction to conduct his funeral according to the customs of lay practitioners meant that if
burial was their tradition, they should bury him; if cre-
mation was their custom, they should cremate him; and
if water burial was their practice, they should perform a
water burial.

The Buddha's funeral was led by the Malla tribe, the royal family of Kushinagar. As the Buddha was of royal lineage, the Mallas cremated the Buddha in accordance with royal traditions.

Hearing of the Buddha's passing, various kingdoms sent emissaries to claim his relics. The Shakyas claimed the Buddha belonged to their tribe, while the Koliyas argued he was their grandson. The people of Vishali said the Buddha had loved their city the most, and King Ajatasattu argued he should enshrine the Buddha's relics because he was one of the Buddha's disciples. The dispute over who would take the relics nearly led to conflict.

At this point, Dona, a Brahmin, intervened, saying, "The Buddha spoke of peace throughout his life. Fighting over the Buddha's relics goes against his teachings. Let us divide them equally into eight parts."

Dona the Brahmin distributed the Buddha's relics among them. They took the relics to their respective countries and built memorial stupas, resulting in eight round stupas.

This marked the conclusion of the Buddha's life. Born as a human, he sought truth, attained enlightenment, and shared the Dharma until his final breath, teaching according to the needs and circumstances of the people. Because of the extraordinary nature of his life, later generations often depicted it symbolically. They described him as a being who had accumulated infinite merit and undertaken countless lifetimes of practice to become the Buddha. Even in the description of his birth, it is symbolically portrayed that he would later renounce the world, become a Buddha, and teach the Dharma to sentient beings.

Although born as a prince in a wealthy and comfortable life, Siddhartha was deeply troubled upon seeing a bird pecking at a worm. Eventually, he renounced the world, devoted himself to practice, and attained enlightenment as Gautama. Sharing his enlightenment with others, he guided people to live without suffering and find happiness. The Buddha was, ultimately, a human being who lived in India 2,600 years ago.

In his life, the Buddha exemplified equality by transcending caste discrimination and gender inequality. He dedicated himself to halting wars and creating a peaceful world. Even in the face of violence and criticism, he maintained equanimity and extended compassion. These facets of the Buddha's character are intricately layered. He demonstrated freedom, equality, peace, and compassion through his words and actions, something that no one else even dreamed of doing in India at the time. Gautama Buddha, who wished for the happiness of all beings, thus became a revolutionary figure far ahead of his time.

02.

Formation of the Buddhist Order and the History of the Spread of the Dharma

●

The First Buddhist Council: Compiling the Sutras and Vinaya

Just as any community experiences shock and disarray after the passing of a great leader, the Buddhist Order faced some confusion after the Buddha entered nirvana. Among the younger practitioners, some reportedly said, "The Buddha used to nag us about what to do and what not to do. Now we can do as we please, right?"

Mahakassapa, a senior disciple, became concerned when he heard this. Recognizing the potential for disorder and misinterpretation over time, he proposed that the Buddha's teachings and precepts be promptly compiled. While many disciples expressed their desire to participate, it was decided that only those who had attained full enlightenment, or arhats, would take part. A total of 500 arhats were selected to assemble at the Saptaparni Cave (Cave of the Seven Leaves), located outside the city of Rajgir to compile the sutras.

To ensure focus and avoid distractions from the general populace, the council convened in an isolated mountain location far from the village. The logistical challenge of going on alms round to obtain food was resolved by the support of King Ajatasattu of Magadha, who provided food offerings for the three-month duration of the council.

The compilation of the sutras, the Buddha's teachings, began with Ananda, who had attended to the Buddha, presenting the first draft. Having attended to the Buddha for 25 years, Ananda had heard the Buddha's teachings more than anyone. He began each recitation with the phrase: "While I was at this place at this time with these people, I heard the Buddha give this teaching." Ananda's accounts adhered strictly to the six principles of inquiry (the five Ws and one H: who, what, when, where, why, and how) to preserve the context and accuracy of the Buddha's teachings.

As Ananda recited, the 500 arhats listened attentively,

either agreeing with the content, suggesting additions where something seemed missing, or proposing corrections if any part seemed inaccurate. Importantly, every decision required unanimous agreement from all 500 arhats to be accepted as authentic.

Once a passage was validated, the group collectively chanted it to ensure it was properly memorized and organized. This meticulous process ensured that the sutras were compiled with remarkable accuracy. Unlike records based on the memory of a single individual, the sutras were the result of thorough deliberation and consensus among 500 enlightened practitioners.

While the sutras are the Buddha's teachings on truth, the Vinaya contains the Buddha's guidelines on practical conduct. The initial draft of the Vinaya was compiled by Upali, a disciple of low-caste origin recognized for his exceptional adherence to the Buddha's teachings. The process of compiling the Vinaya mirrored that of the sutras: each rule was presented, and unanimous agreement from the assembly was required for its acceptance. In this manner, the sutras, the Buddha's teachings on truth, and the Vinaya, the Buddha's guidance on practical conduct, were compiled during the First Buddhist Council.

However, among those who could not participate in the council, some objected to the compiled sutras and Vinaya. The Buddha had anticipated such issues and had provided a principle for future disputes: "After I enter nirvana, if someone claims that they heard certain teachings from the Buddha or a senior disciple, neither accept it unconditionally nor reject it outright. Listen carefully to the claim and compare it against the officially verified sutras and Vinaya. If the content aligns with them, accept it. If it does not, reject it."

Initially, the 500 disciples of the Buddha had slightly differing views. However, since most of them had been directly inspired by the Buddha, the compilation of the sutras and Vinaya proceeded relatively smoothly. This was the First Buddhist Council.

●

The Second Buddhist Council: Addressing Claims Reflecting Social Changes

A century after the Buddha's passing, the number of practitioners had significantly increased, and the Buddhist order had grown in size. Along with these developments, societal changes brought about objections to certain aspects of the Vinaya.

During the Buddha's time, ordained practitioners owned no possessions, wore only pamsukula robes, and relied solely on alms for food. However, with the advent of commerce and the use of currency, the question of whether monks could accept money was raised.

The initial issue concerned whether monks could store salt for future use. This later escalated into a larger debate about whether it was permissible for monks to accept money. For instance, if a merchant wanted to make an offering but gave money because they had no food in hand, wouldn't it be equivalent to offering food if the money was used to buy food? A total of ten specific issues were raised at the time, especially by monks from the progressive city of Vaishali.

To address these concerns, 700 elders gathered in Vaishali a hundred years after the Buddha's passing to deliberate on these matters. Regarding the sutras, some previously omitted teachings were acknowledged and added. However, when it came to the Vinaya, the elders adopted a strict stance. All ten suggestions reflecting the changing circumstances of the time were rejected. This rigid approach created a division between the conservative elders, who led the council, and the younger, more progressive monks advocating for change. This marked the Second Buddhist Council. Like the First Council, it relied entirely on oral transmission rather than written records.

●

The Third Buddhist Council: Establishing the Foundations of Early Buddhism with the Tripitaka

A century passed after the Second Buddhist Council. After unifying India, King Ashoka converted to Buddhism and dispatched missionaries worldwide to spread the Dharma. However, by this time, the Buddhist order had fragmented into numerous sects due to disagreements over the Vinaya, leading to discord within the Sangha. To resolve these issues, King Ashoka convened the Third Buddhist Council, assembling 1,000 elders at a monastery within his palace in Pataliputra, the capital of his empire.

During the Third Buddhist Council, in addition to compiling the sutras and Vinaya, Abhidharma—commentaries and analyses—were organized. With the changing times, it became necessary to interpret the sutras and Vinaya in a way that was relevant to contemporary society. Many prominent monks contributed their interpretations, and among these, the interpretations that were officially recognized became part of the Abhidharma. Thus, the Buddhist canon came to consist of three parts: the sutras, the Vinaya, and the Abhidharma. This tripartite collection, known as the Tripitaka, became the foundation of early Buddhism. Similarly, Korea's Tripitaka Koreana from the Goryeo Dynasty also includes the sutras, Vinaya, and Abhidharma.

Over time, increasingly divergent interpretations of the sutras and Vinaya led to debates, despite the Buddha's explicit teaching against engaging in them. As Buddhism spread to new regions, regional differences gave rise to distinct sects.

Initially, the Sangha divided into two schools: Theravada (Sthaviravada or Sect of Elders), which emphasized the strict adherence to the Buddha's original teachings, and the Mahasamghika (Great Community), which advocated for flexibility and adaptation to the changing times. This division of the once-unified Buddhist order into two schools is referred to as the First Schism. Over time, further subdivisions occurred within both the

Theravada and Mahasamghika schools. Throughout history, various sects emerged and disappeared, and a total of about 20 sects were formed.

Some sects grew large, while others remained small. Each claimed to be the most legitimate and authentic representation of the Buddha's teachings. As a result, individual sects revised the sutras, wrote new Abhidharma to rationalize their revisions, and redefined the Vinaya. These efforts to solidify and defend their positions led to variations in emphasis and practice across sects, despite their shared origin in the Buddha's teachings.

For monks, the primary focus shifted to memorizing the Buddha's words and studying the Abhidharma specific to their sect. This intensive education often required decades of study, leaving little time to engage with lay followers to awaken them from ignorance and alleviate their suffering. Supported by patrons who built temples and provided accommodations, monks often dedicated all their time to scholarly pursuits. Over time, their roles diverged into two categories: one as religious leaders, offering prayers and blessings, and the other as scholar, specializing in the study of Buddhist doctrines.

As a result, the role of monks in comforting and guiding lay followers diminished. Observing this, many lay practitioners felt a disconnect between the Buddha's teachings and the behavior of the monks. In response, lay people began forming their own faith communities, centered on remembering the Buddha and supporting one another. This movement led to the emergence of a new form of Buddhism, known as Mahayana Buddhism.

The traditional monastic community criticized the Mahayana movement, labeling it as non-authentic teachings. In turn, Mahayana Buddhists referred to their tradition as the "Great Vehicle," implying that traditional Buddhism, or Hinayana, was the "Lesser Vehicle."

It is important to note that the terms "Mahayana" and "Hinayana" originated within the Mahayana tradition and were not agreed upon by both sides. In modern contexts, countries like Korea, which follow the Mahayana tradition, often refer to Theravada as "Hinayana." However, from the perspective of Theravada Buddhists, they view themselves as the foundational and authentic form of Buddhism, while they regard Mahayana as non-authentic.

●

The Spread of Buddhism
Beyond India

After the rise of Mahayana Buddhism in India, both Mahayana and Theravada Buddhism spread to other regions. Theravada Buddhism expanded southward to countries such as Thailand, Sri Lanka, Myanmar, Laos, Cambodia, southern Vietnam, Malaysia, and Indonesia. Meanwhile, both Mahayana and Theravada Buddhism entered China, but over time, Mahayana Buddhism became more dominant due to its compatibility with Chinese culture, leading to the gradual decline of Theravada Buddhism in the region. Consequently, China, Korea, Japan, and Vietnam became part of the Mahayana Buddhist sphere.

Initially, the Mahayana movement aimed to return to the original teachings of the Buddha. The Buddha had said: "Truth cannot be validated solely by traditions, morality, customs, habits, precepts, or sutras handed down from the past." Based on this teaching, Mahayana Buddhism asserted that any rigid definition of "truth" itself would contradict the essence of truth. Even the teachings and doctrines themselves are considered "empty." They emphasized that accepting anything as fixed or unchanging goes against the Buddha's teachings, including the very Dharma itself. This idea of "emptiness" became the central philosophy of Mahayana Buddhism.

When Buddhism first arrived in China, it faced significant challenges. However, it began to flourish rapidly during the Southern and Northern Dynasties. In the Southern Dynasties, particularly during the Liang Dynasty, Buddhism received strong state support from the royal family. During the Sui and Tang Dynasties, Buddhism became the central religion of the country.

Initially, the Chinese found it difficult to understand Buddhism and often interpreted it through the lens of Taoism, which shared some similarities with Buddhism. This interpretative approach was called Geyi Buddhism. However, by the Sui and Tang periods, the Chinese were able to embrace Buddhism on its own terms, without relying on Taoist analogies.

Over time, Mahayana Buddhism in China diversified into several schools. These included the Huayan School, centered on the *Avatamsaka Sutra*, and the Tiantai School, which focused on the *Lotus Sutra*. Buddhism evolved along two main paths, one emphasizing devotional practices for accumulating merit and blessings, and the other focusing on academic study and philosophical development.

Amid these changes, a new movement advocating a return to the direct experience of the Buddha's teachings arose. This movement was Seon Buddhism (also known as Chan Buddhism in China and Zen Buddhism in Japan). Seon Buddhism critiqued the existing Buddhist schools, referring to them collectively as "doctrinal teachings" and claimed that the "Seon" they advocated represented the true essence of the Buddha's teachings. They declared: "Seon is the Buddha's mind, and the Teachings are the Buddha's words."

Asserting the value of Seon over doctrinal teachings, Seon Buddhism emphasized "non-reliance on words and letters." It claimed that truth cannot be expressed through language and writing but must be directly experienced in the mind. Seon teachings highlight the concept of "directly pointing to the human mind, seeing one's nature, and becoming a Buddha," that is, self-awareness is equivalent to becoming a Buddha.

Mahayana Buddhism taught that one could only become a Buddha through countless acts of compassion and merit accumulation over many lifetimes, making it nearly impossible for an ordinary person to become a

Buddha. So, when Seon radically proposed that you can become a Buddha by simply knowing your mind, it was initially dismissed as heretical.

Mahayana thrived during times of political stability, when the state supported Buddhism, built temples, and made offerings to monks. Conversely, during chaotic periods, such as regime changes and anti-Buddhist policies, Seon Buddhism gained prominence for its focus on maintaining equanimity of the mind, while the doctrinal schools lost state support and declined. This historical shift allowed Seon Buddhism to become the dominant school in China and the rest of East Asia.

In Korea, Seon Buddhism became mainstream not solely through the efforts of the Seon practitioners but also due to state-imposed reforms. During the Joseon Dynasty, which actively suppressed Buddhism, many sects were forcibly consolidated. The doctrinal schools were merged into one sect, while the Nine Mountain Schools of Seon were unified under a single Seon sect. Thus, Buddhism became largely divided into two main schools: the Seon school and the doctrinal school. Later, these two branches were forcibly unified into a single tradition, the Jogye Order, making Seon the dominant school in Korea.

Buddhism was first introduced to Korea by Venerable Jangyu Hwasang during the Gaya Confederacy period. Although this claim has not yet been academically recognized, it is believed to have occurred in 48 CE, predating Buddhism's introduction to China. Official records show that from China, Buddhism entered Goguryeo in 372 CE and Baekje in 384 CE. From Goguryeo, it entered Silla, spreading throughout the Korean Peninsula. During the Unified Silla period, Buddhism flourished with the establishment of the Five Doctrinal Schools and the Nine Mountain Schools of Seon. During the Goryeo Dynasty, Buddhism became the state religion, with the development of 11 schools, including Cheontae and Seon.

However, as Buddhism became corrupt in late Goryeo, the new scholar-officials who led the dynastic revolution embraced Neo-Confucianism and rejected Buddhism. Buddhism faced extreme persecution throughout the 500 years of the Joseon Dynasty. Few religious traditions in history have experienced suppression as severe or prolonged as Korean Buddhism during this era. Today, Korean Buddhism faces the task of overcoming the past wounds and integrating with modern civilization to offer new solutions for humanity's future.

●

Emergence of
Various Buddhist Movements
in Conjunction with
the Changing Times

Today, Buddhism has expanded beyond India and the East to merge with Western civilization. Various movements have emerged worldwide, seeking to return to the Buddha's original teachings while incorporating ideologies such as women's liberation and class emancipation. The most notable example is the Navayana (New Buddhism) movement led by Dr. B.R. Ambedkar in India.

Ambedkar was born a Dalit (formerly referred to as "untouchables") but studied in Britain, became a leader in the Indian independence movement, and served as India's first law minister. Ambedkar stands alongside Gandhi as a pivotal figure in India's struggle for independence. However, while Gandhi focused solely on India's independence from British rule, Ambedkar argued that true liberation must be accompanied by class liberation. He asserted that independence was meaningless for Dalits if the new nation retained its oppressive caste system.

Since Hinduism upheld the caste hierarchy, he converted to Buddhism, believing that genuine class liberation
would not be achieved as long as people were faithful to
Hinduism.

People from his caste and those who have inherited
his vision, continue to unite in advancing the Navayana
Buddhist movement, which strongly advocates for class
liberation. Even in contemporary Korean Buddhism, beliefs such as the concept of reincarnation, the theory of
karma from past lives, and retributive justice are evident,
reflecting the influence of traditional Indian culture.
Ambedkar's Navayana movement strongly opposes these
ideas, instead advocating for the original teachings of the
Buddha, centered on compassion and equality, as a philosophy of liberation for the people. The Navayana Buddhist movement in India is a uniquely Indian approach
to class and social liberation through Buddhism, distinct
from the class liberation ideology of socialism.

There are also various other Buddhist movements.
One notable example is the nonviolent peace movement led by the Dalai Lama, which symbolizes Tibet's
resistance against Chinese occupation. Although Tibet's
struggle for national liberation has the potential to escalate into armed conflict, the Dalai Lama advocates

resolving the issue peacefully, following the teachings of the Buddha.

In Taiwan, the Tzu Chi Foundation was founded by Bhikkhuni Cheng Yen. With over 4 million volunteers in Taiwan and additional support from the global Chinese community, it has become the world's largest volunteer organization. It is large enough to operate hospitals and broadcasting stations, as well as manage an environmental program focused on nationwide waste sorting and recycling. Tzu Chi is leading a new Buddhist movement rooted in volunteerism and environmentalism.

In Thailand, the Santi Asoke community embodies a self-reliant lifestyle, refusing donations and striving to harmonize farming with Buddhist practice. They do not perform religious rituals in exchange for compensation but instead live a self-sufficient life centered on practice. This relatively new community produces, sells, and distributes organic crops.

The late Thich Nhat Hanh, a renowned Vietnamese monk, led a global anti-war peace movement opposing the Vietnam War. Following the war, he devoted his life to spreading practices that cultivate inner peace worldwide.

Across the globe, various movements have emerged with a shared goal of returning to the Buddha's original teachings. Just as the Buddha charted a new path by integrating various different thoughts in India during his time, these modern Buddhist movements, situated within the complexities of science, technology, social sciences, traditional culture, the meeting of East and West, and various religions, must forge a path for future civilization based on the Buddha's teachings.

The greatest challenge for Buddhism moving forward is to find solutions in the Buddha's teachings to address the problem of human suffering that persists even amidst the abundance of material civilization.

03.

If You Free Yourself from Anguish, You Are a Buddha

●

Everyone Can Be Happy

So far, we have examined the life of the Buddha and the history of Buddhism after the Buddha's passing. The most important thing for us in this process is to consider what life lessons we can learn from Gautama Buddha, who lived 2,600 years ago.

One of the Buddha's teachings is that "Everyone can become a Buddha." This is often expressed as "Everyone possesses Buddha-nature." However, this phrase can lead to the misunderstanding that there is an innate "self," like a diamond, called Buddha-nature within us. If we say there is such a self, it aligns with the concept of Atman in Upanishadic philosophy. However, the Buddha's core teaching is the doctrine of non-self—the idea that there is no permanent, unchanging self.

Then, what does it mean that everyone can become a Buddha? It means that everyone can be free from suffering and attain happiness. The central goal of the Buddha's teachings is liberation and nirvana. Liberation means being free from all bondage, and nirvana means the cessation of all suffering. Nirvana is the state in which all suffering has disappeared, a state without suffering. Simply put, it is a state of sustainable happiness.

The happiness we generally talk about is one that inevitably turns into unhappiness. When we desire something and achieve it, we feel good. However, if we base our happiness on this feeling of pleasure, we must also endure the inevitable counterpart—unhappiness. Such happiness is not sustainable.

Sustainable happiness, on the other hand, is a state free from suffering, a state of nirvana. It is a happiness that does not fluctuate between joy and suffering. What does it mean to be healthy? Is it the ability to lift a certain weight or run at great speed? No, being healthy means not being sick. Similarly, happiness means being free from suffering. Just as health is the absence of illness, true happiness is the absence of suffering.

Everyone can achieve this state of being free from suffering. However, we always rationalize our suffering by blaming others—our husband, wife, children, parents, or financial situation. We spend our energy tormenting ourselves and rationalize our suffering by convincing ourselves that we have no choice but to be unhappy.

However, with a little introspection, we can shift our perspective. For example, when someone insults you, ask yourself, "Why do I get angry when that person curses at me? Why do I suffer when that person says such things?"

Through such self-examination, we can realize that it wasn't something to suffer over. We may understand that the person spoke out of their own anger or perspective. If we fail to understand their situation, we may feel anger or frustration. But when we do understand, the frustration dissipates, and we feel at ease.

"Oh, that's why they said those things."

When we do not understand why someone behaves a certain way, we wonder, "Why are they doing that?" and feel frustrated. However, once we understand them, the frustration disappears.

"Ah, that's why they acted that way."

We often believe that our suffering stems from others not understanding our feelings. But upon closer analysis, it becomes clear that our suffering arises when we fail to understand others.

●

There Is No Suffering in a Loving Heart

We often say that we are suffering because we are not loved. In reality, we suffer not because we are not loved, but because we do not love. This is a common misunderstanding. A loving heart is free from suffering. Yet, when we love, we often treat it as an investment or a transaction.

"I love you, so you should love me too."

This means the goal is not in loving but in being loved. We suffer in life when the desire to be loved isn't fulfilled or when the help we seek is not given.

During marriage counseling, it becomes evident how couples' feelings toward each other change over time. Before getting married, they choose their partner thinking, "I will benefit from this marriage." However, after having lived together for a while, they might realize, "There's not much to gain here" and eventually question the value of the marriage, concluding that the relationship is a net loss. Even marital relationships are driven by self-interest. When people view their spouse as an investment, they begin to feel resentful and suffer if they perceive that what they give is greater than what they receive.

However, if we love our partner as we might love a flower, a mountain, or the sea, suffering does not arise. We don't expect the mountain to acknowledge our admiration, nor do we demand the sea to understand our affection. In such relationships, love does not turn into suffering.

Instead of seeking to be loved,
love.
Instead of wanting to be understood,
seek to understand.
Instead of waiting for help,
offer it.
Instead of looking for someone to lean on,
be a source of support.

Then, there is no reason for you to suffer because of others.

●

When You Understand
the Principles of the Mind,
Suffering Disappears

Imagine two people working in a field. From a distance, it is difficult to tell who is the master and who is the laborer. But upon closer observation, it becomes clear: the one who gives money to the other and says, "Thank you for your work today," is the master.

The one who gives is the owner, while the one who tries to receive is a servant or a hired hand. Similarly, the one who wishes to rely on others, be loved, be understood, and receive help is a sentient being.

Sentient beings create their own suffering through their ignorance. Our suffering does not arise from sins committed in a past life, punishment from a deity, or horoscopes and destiny. Marital conflicts do not occur because of poor astrological compatibility but because they insist on their own opinions and fight over self-interests.

If we acknowledge that others are different from us, conflicts will not arise. Recognizing and accepting differences in beliefs, personalities, thoughts, judgments, values, and preferences as they are—that is respect. We should go one step further to understand those differences.

"From their perspective, that might make sense."

"From their viewpoint, it's possible to say those things and act that way."

Understanding someone does not mean agreeing that they are always right. It means acknowledging that their perspective might lead them to think or act in a particular way. When we can do this, we will no longer become angry due to others' actions or words.

Practice is not about suppressing the negative feelings that arise in our hearts. Rather, when we acknowledge and understand those who are different from us, we have no reason to resent them. When we understand how the mind works, practice becomes much simpler. When the Buddha was insulted, he responded with a gentle smile because he understood the thoughts and motivations behind the person's words. Similarly, if we wish to free ourselves from suffering and live as liberated individuals, we must first understand the principles of the mind. By grasping this truth, we can live without stress and lead a happy life.

Most of the issues we face are relative. Even if we have enough to live on, we compare ourselves to others. If we have more money than someone else, we consider ourselves wealthy. This reflects the Buddha's words: "building your happiness on the misfortune of others." Unfortunately, this is how many of us live today.

Moreover, we continue to discriminate against others. Being born a woman or with a disability is not a sin. Being poor is not a sin either. Yet, we often rationalize these situations by claiming they are the results of misdeeds in past lives. This mindset perpetuates the justification of poverty and discrimination. We mistakenly view our own internalized discriminations as objective truths due to errors in our perception.

However, the essence of all beings lies in their unique characteristics, and we should accept them as they are. The Buddha taught us that even though discrimination exists in our reality, all beings are simply different, not inherently superior or inferior, right or wrong. It is our mistaken perception that leads us to think that there is a legitimate reason for discrimination. Justice can be called the process of moving from discrimination to equality.

Studying the Buddha's teachings may not solve all of society's problems, but understanding his teachings can help us let go of rigid values and fixed beliefs. By doing so, we might be able to abandon the habit of insisting that only our perspective is correct and begin to recognize and respect the perspectives of others.

As we learn the Buddha's teachings, it is important to put them into practice where improvements are needed. The first step is to adhere to the precepts and follow the right path. Secondly, we need to be patient with others. This does not mean simply letting them be, but understanding that, just as we sometimes struggle to achieve something even when we know how, they may face similar challenges. We feel a sense of peace when we can patiently watch over others. Finally, we must put in consistent effort to make improvement.

●

Social Foundation Is Essential for Personal Happiness

Everyone born into this world has the right to happiness. To live happily, both individual practice and social action are necessary. Humans do not live in isolation; they exist in communities such as families and societies, interacting with others. The Buddha outlined six conditions for achieving harmony within a community. Merely talking about harmony does not make it happen. When harmony breaks down, it is always because at least one of these six conditions is not being met.

The first condition is that everyone must adhere to the same precepts. If ten people live together, the same rules must apply equally to all. If rules are applied selectively, it leads to discrimination and conflict. In modern terms, this is akin to the principle of "All people are equal before the law."

The second condition is to gather and engage in discussions frequently. This principle aligns with the idea of democracy. Since people have different views and thoughts, they need to have regular discussions and make collective decisions. If one person makes unilateral decisions, misunderstandings and dissatisfaction can arise, reducing the sense of responsibility among group members.

The third condition is to share alms and offerings equally. In modern terms, this corresponds to economic equality. In a community, if some have more than others, or if some have better quality resources than others, dissatisfaction is inevitable. Economic equality within the community is crucial, as inequality inevitably leads to conflict.

The fourth condition is to live together as a community, not separately. Living together fosters transparency, as everyone can observe one another, reducing misunderstandings and misgivings. In modern terms, this can be related to equality in opportunity, fairness in processes, and equitable distribution of outcomes. Opportunities must be provided equally, processes must be fair, and the distribution of results should be acceptable to all.

The fifth condition is to always speak gently and compassionately, with a smile. Since people communicate through words, if sharp words or criticism are used in the community, conflicts will arise. Kind and considerate speech is essential for harmony. Words hold immense power in fostering or disrupting harmony.

Finally, the sixth condition is to respect others' perspectives. This means not fixating on what is right or wrong but instead recognizing, "From their perspective, they may have a point." It is about acknowledging the differences in others. In a diverse society like Korea, where multiple religions coexist, respecting others' beliefs is vital. Similarly, when cultural or ideological differences arise, recognizing and respecting them is essential.

Faith, religion, ideology, and belief systems are deeply personal matters and should not be imposed on others.

If these six conditions are realized, wouldn't much of the confrontation and conflict in our society disappear? The Buddha's teachings are not confined to a specific region or era; they remain relevant and applicable to all modern societies and communities.

It's commonly believed that concepts like democracy, equality, and respect for human rights originated in the West, but these principles were inherently present in the Buddha's teachings. The Buddha introduced them 2,600 years ago, and they were even partially practiced in society at the time. Unfortunately, their continuation was hindered during the medieval feudal era, when patriarchal systems and caste hierarchies distorted the Buddha's teachings.

●

Meeting
the Revolutionary Buddha

The current era of democratization and freedom is the ideal time for the Buddha's original teachings to be directly applied to people's lives. This is because we live in a time when what is most just can also become the most universal. Moreover, in today's world, which is materially abundant yet spiritually lacking, the Buddha's teachings may serve as an alternative to address our shortcomings.

Through a modern lens, I have reexamined the Buddha—a compassionate figure to the marginalized, a bold revolutionary who transcended his time, and an individual who lived as a practitioner. Though I initially encountered Buddhism in my youth, I became disillusioned with its institutional realities at one point. However, studying the Buddha's life reignited my faith in his teachings.

By exploring the historical and social context of the Buddha's life, stripping away the mythological and exaggerated narratives, and viewing him from a cultural and historical perspective, I realized that the Buddha was indeed a true revolutionary. He was not a revolutionary who sought to change society through physical force but a spiritual revolutionary who awakened people from ignorance and opened the door to a new world. He was, indeed, a great revolutionary.

I hope the readers of this book will not view the "revolutionary Buddha" I have discovered as only a practitioner. Instead, I hope you will use the lessons of the Buddha's life as a mirror to reflect upon your own life. I conclude this writing by asking you to think deeply about how we should live our lives now, and to ponder the question of how to tackle the current issues of the disintegration of our communities, the distortion of self, and the destruction of the global environment.

About the Author

Ven. Pomnyun Sunim

Ven. Pomnyun Sunim is a peace activist who delivers messages of peace and reconciliation, a humanitarian activist who provides various forms of aid to developing countries, a thinker who is paving the way toward a new alternative civilization, and an awakened practitioner. In 1988, he founded the Jungto Society, a community of practitioners who vowed to free themselves from suffering and devote themselves to serving others and the world by leading the life of a bodhisattva.

Ven. Pomnyun Sunim's Dharma talks are clear and straightforward. He has an exceptional ability to explain the Buddha's teachings in simple, contemporary language. As a result, his spoken and written messages go straight to the heart of the matter and enable people to redirect their eyes inward and self-reflect. Furthermore, the esoteric content of Buddhist sutras come to life through his wisdom, intuition, and insight.

As of April 2022, YouTube videos of Sumin's Dharma talks have had more than 1.7 billion views. He shares his wisdom with the general public on how to free themselves from suffering and how to become happy through his Dharma Q&As and the Happiness School program. To date, he has delivered more than 12,000 Dharma Q&As in South Korea and about 300 Dharma Q&As in other countries around the world, including the 115 talks he gave during his global tour in 2014. Also, since the Covid-19 pandemic began in 2020, Ven. Pomnyun Sunim has been interacting with hundreds of thousands of people through his weekly online Dharma Q&As in Korean, and bi-weekly talks in English. (See his website: https://pomnyun.com/)

Among the more than 50 books Ven. Pomnyun Sunim has published in Korean so far, the most notable are *Things Are Good as They Are Now*, *Buddha*, and *Commentary on the Diamond Sutra*. His books encompass a

wide range of subjects. His books, *Words of Wisdom for Newlyweds*, *Becoming Happier*, and *I Am a Decent Person*, provide insightful advice to young people. *Lessons for Life* is a guidebook for people living in modern society. *Prayer: Letting Go* is a manual for lay practitioners. *Practice Guidebook for Teachers* imparts wisdom for teachers. *The River of Life Flows* discusses an alternative solution to the environmental problem. And *Why Is Unification Necessary?* offers a vision for peace and unification on the Korean peninsula.

Some of these books have been translated into other languages, such as English, French, Thai, Japanese, Chinese, and Vietnamese. Eight books have been translated into English, including *Awakening*, *True Freedom*, *Prayer*, and *Monk's Reply to Everyday Problems* to list a few. Six books have been translated into Chinese, three books into Thai, two books into Japanese, two books into Vietnamese, and one book into French. Among the few books that were translated into multiple languages is *My Happy Way to Work*, which was translated into Thai, Chinese, Japanese, and Vietnamese. Another is *Becoming Happier*, which has English, Vietnamese, and Japanese versions.

Based on the idea that practice at the individual level goes hand in hand with social engagement, Ven. Pomnyun Sunim has engaged in extensive peace initiatives for various causes including a peaceful unification of the Korean Peninsula, refugee support, international relief efforts, and interfaith reconciliation and cooperation. Throughout the years, he has received numerous awards in recognition for his efforts. In 2002, he received the Ramon Magsaysay Award for Peace and International Understanding, and he was presented the 37th Niwano Peace Prize in 2021.

The Buddha—
A True Revolutionary

©Ven. Pomnyun Sunim, 2025

First Edition   30, April, 2025
Published by   Jungto Publishing
                42 Hyoryeong-ro 51-gil, Seocho-gu, Seoul, Korea
                tel. +82-2-587-8991
                e-mail. jungtobook@gmail.com
Written by   Ven. Pomnyun Sunim
Translated by   Jungto International Translation Team
Design by   Design Studio Dongkyong

ISBN: 979-11-87297-83-3 (03220)
Printed in the Republic of Korea.

US $25 ₩20,000